World War Aid

World War Aid offers a novel perspective on the unprecedented aid in the Ukrainian conflict, destined to leave an international "echo" reaching far beyond the individual historical case and the aid sector alone.

This book clarifies the evolving scenario of a conflict that, before tanks, had long been fought on the territory of aid. The author makes arguments about aid which can be traced back to three sets of issues: (1) Ukraine's history from its independence in 1991 until the war in 2022, that witnessed the evolution of interstate aid sent to Kyiv. This period anticipated the geo-political dispute over the country's future, and was marked by confrontation between donors who would later become the protagonists of the war scenario. (2) The exceptionality of the Ukrainian case is discussed by specifically identifying eight peculiarities of wartime aid: the response speed of Western Bilateral Donors; the leading role and primacy of the latter over the non-governmental sector; the key influence exercised by the Ukrainian recipient; the quantity and diversification of aid involved; Russia's conversion of aid into hybrid weapons (*Weaponization of Aid*); the West's provision of weapons as primary aid (*Aidization of Weapons*); the excessive anticipation of post-war planning initiatives; and sanctions modeled to represent a new form of aid. (3) Based on these peculiarities, a new model of *Interventionist Aid* is defined, characterized by a willingness to take an active part in the crisis in which the Donors operate, in order to condition its course and outcome. By preferring tactical purposes to humanitarian ones, and prioritizing military and financial interventions, *Interventionist Aid* represents an absolute conceptual, political and historical novelty in interstate aid.

A highly original take on a key event of the twenty-first century, *World War Aid* is an invaluable text for political scientists, analysts and historians of international relations, as well as diplomats and practitioners of foreign policy and foreign aid.

Igor Pellicciari is a full professor of History of International Institutions and Relations at the University of Urbino Carlo Bo, Italy. A senior EU expert on aid to transition countries, he is also a diplomat of the Republic of San Marino, currently Ambassador to the Kingdom of Jordan. He consulted on the Sputnik V vaccine deal that made San Marino the first Covid-free state in the world. He is author of *Re-Framing Foreign Aid History and Politics* (Routledge, 2022).

Innovations in International Affairs
Series Editor: Raffaele Marchetti, *LUISS Guido Carli, Italy*

Innovations in International Affairs aims to provide cutting-edge analyses of controversial trends in international affairs with the intent to innovate our understanding of global politics. Hosting mainstream as well as alternative stances, the series promotes both the re-assessment of traditional topics and the exploration of new aspects.

The series invites both engaged scholars and reflective practitioners, and is committed to bringing non-western voices into current debates.

Innovations in International Affairs is keen to consider new book proposals in the following key areas:

- **Innovative topics**: related to aspects that have remained marginal in scholarly and public debates
- **International crises**: related to the most urgent contemporary phenomena and how to interpret and tackle them
- **World perspectives**: related mostly to non-western points of view.

Titles in this series include:

World War Aid
Interventionist Aid and War in Ukraine
Igor Pellicciari

For more information about this series, please visit: www.routledge.com/Innovations-in-International-Affairs/book-series/IIA

World War Aid
Interventionist Aid and War in Ukraine

Igor Pellicciari

Routledge
Taylor & Francis Group

LONDON AND NEW YORK

First published 2024
by Routledge
4 Park Square, Milton Park, Abingdon, Oxon OX14 4RN

and by Routledge
605 Third Avenue, New York, NY 10158

Routledge is an imprint of the Taylor & Francis Group, an informa business

© 2024 Igor Pellicciari

The right of Igor Pellicciari to be identified as author of this work has been asserted in accordance with sections 77 and 78 of the Copyright, Designs and Patents Act 1988.

All rights reserved. No part of this book may be reprinted or reproduced or utilized in any form or by any electronic, mechanical, or other means, now known or hereafter invented, including photocopying and recording, or in any information storage or retrieval system, without permission in writing from the publishers.

Published with the contribution of the University of Urbino Carlo Bo; LINK University; Policy Advice Projects s.r.l.

Text edited by the Author with the stylistic assistance from Catherine Lea Farwell (University of Urbino Carlo Bo).

Trademark Notice: Product or corporate names may be trademarks or registered trademarks, and are used only for identification and explanation without intent to infringe.

British Library Cataloguing-in-Publication Data
A catalogue record for this book is available from the British Library

Library of Congress Cataloging-in-Publication Data
Names: Pellicciari, Igor, author.
Title: World war aid : interventionist aid and war in Ukraine / Igor Pellicciari.
Description: 1. | New York : Routledge, 2023. |
Series: Innovations in international affairs |
Includes bibliographical references and index.
Identifiers: LCCN 2023036072 (print) | LCCN 2023036073 (ebook) |
ISBN 9781032465340 (hardback) | ISBN 9781032465357 (paperback) |
ISBN 9781003382157 (ebook)
Subjects: LCSH: Military assistance–Ukraine. |
Military assistance–Russia (Federation) |
Ukraine–History–Russian Invasion, 2022–
Classification: LCC DK508.852 .P365 2023 (print) |
LCC DK508.852 (ebook) | DDC 355.032477–dc23/eng/20230831
LC record available at https://lccn.loc.gov/2023036072
LC ebook record available at https://lccn.loc.gov/2023036073

ISBN: 978-1-032-46534-0 (hbk)
ISBN: 978-1-032-46535-7 (pbk)
ISBN: 978-1-003-38215-7 (ebk)

DOI: 10.4324/9781003382157

Typeset in Times New Roman
by Newgen Publishing UK

This book is dedicated to all civilian victims of war.

Contents

Foreword   xii
ROMANO PRODI

1   Interventionist Aid   1
      True Aid Revolution 1
      Key Conclusions and Findings of This Book 5
      Ex-Ante Disclaimer: The Sense of This Book 11

2   Aid Connecting Virus and War   14
      Aid, a Mainstream Word 14
      International Aid Public Policies to Compare Pandemic and War 18
      Framing Aid in the Ukrainian War 20

3   Ukrainian War Symptoms in Aid History   23
      Aid to Ukraine (1991–2022) 23
      1991–2004 Aid without Reform 26
      2005–2010 The Pro-European Ambition 31
      2010–2014 Aid War 35
      2014–2022 The Atlanticist Strategy 37

4   From Neutralist to Interventionist Aid   48
      Ukraine 2022 vs Bosnia and Herzegovina 1992 48
      Bosnia and Herzegovina 1992: A Perfect Storm 50
      Neutralist Aid 55
      Ukraine 2022: A Big Game Scenario 58
      International Relevance 58

    Incidence of Exogenous Factors 61
    Consolidated Ukrainian Statehood 62
    Classic Military Warfare 63
    Unprecedented Aid in the War in Ukraine 64
    Donor–Recipient Peculiarities 65
    Aid Peculiarities 66
    Peculiarities in the Strategic Approach Adopted 66
    Neutralist Aid vs Interventionist Aid 67

5 Peculiarities of Interventionist Aid   70
    The First Peculiarity: Response Speed of Western Bilateral Donors 70
    The Second Peculiarity: Leading Role and Primacy of Western Bilateral Donors 74
    The Third Peculiarity: The Recipient-Partner 77
    The Fourth Peculiarity: Quantity and Diversification of Aid 82
    The Fifth Peculiarity: Aid Turned into Hybrid Weapons (Weaponization of Aid) 88
    The Sixth Peculiarity: Weapons as Primary Aid (Aidization of Weapons) 92
    The Seventh Peculiarity: Premature Opening of the Post-conflict Phase 96
    The Eighth Peculiarity: Sanctions as Aid (Aidization of Sanctions) 103

6 Interventionist Aid vs Pandemic Aid   110
    Scenario: Aid as a Central Driver of International Relations 110
    Actors: Rise of the Bilateral Donor 112
    Aid: Weapons and Vaccines to Change the Course of Events 115

7 The Interventionist Aid Revolution: Political, Conceptual, Historical   121
    The Political Dimension: New Interventionist Aid 121
    The Conceptual Dimension: Anarchical Aid as a Key Component of War 124
    The Historical Dimension: The New "Interventionist Aid Phase" 128

Postscript: The (Possible) Future of
Interventionist Aid   131
Interventionist Aid World Order 132
Post-Democracy Aid 133
World War Aid 136

Bibliography   *139*
Index   *146*

Foreword

With a focus on international aid in the war in Ukraine, this book adds an original key to understanding one of the most dramatic events of our time.

Along with a historical reconstruction of three decades of aid from the same donors that faced off in the 2022 conflict, the new features of aid in the first year of the conflict are identified here, representing a true turning point from the past.

Identifying the historical symptoms of today's conflict in the "Aid War" previously fought by donors and describing eight technical-political peculiarities regarding the aid system, the present work emphasizes how new practices of *Interventionist Aid* manifested itself in Ukraine to counter the Russian military invasion. Subsequently juxtaposition of *Interventionist Aid* with the *Neutralist Humanitarian and Development Cooperation Aid* predominant in other scenarios of past decades is carried out.

Anticipated in some respects by *Vaccine Diplomacy* aid during the pandemic, in reality *Interventionist Aid* defines a new model of donor action that aims to determine the outcome of the crisis in which it operates; if necessary the latter objectives require the placement of tactical-political goals before humanitarian ones.

This work analyses the aforesaid from a new perspective, alternating between a political, conceptual and historical dimension that stimulates the reader to compare in critical terms the resultant picture of a radical reorganization of the aid system.

Personally, these pages prompted some considerations related to my academic and political experience.

On the research side, this book contributes to the interdisciplinary study of aid policies; although the topic is experiencing increasing fortune in the scholarly literature, the aforesaid continues to be treated with a polarized approach ranging from purely theoretical considerations in International Relations to the quantitative empirical analyses of economists.

After a lifetime spent studying and putting industrial policies into practice, I cannot but appreciate an approach that considers the study of aid policies not only in terms of classic Foreign Aid, but also of economic and financial interventions. Furthermore, this is done without idealizing them *a priori*. This is necessary precisely to prevent that the future reconstruction of Ukraine take place via the replaying of scenarios from the past, in which the donors who managed the aid benefited more than the recipients who received it.

On the political level, this book led me to question once again how it was possible that matters in Ukraine could take such a tragic turn, and how a Russian military invasion could occur, leaving us incredulous and dismayed, taking us back to war scenarios that we thought had finally been exorcised, at least in Europe.

In 2004, without a single shot being fired, four countries from the former Warsaw Pact and three others that had been part of the former USSR joined the EU; meanwhile today, Ukraine and its citizens find themselves having to pay a huge price in terms of loss of life and destruction of the country to achieve their legitimate European aspirations. As a direct witness of the former season, I can state that – at that time – enlargement took place without opposition from Moscow. Indeed, it happened thanks to Russia's convergence on European positions. Considering today's tragic developments, one suspects that Russia's actions at the time were just tactics. However, the benefits for the European Union were tangible, and furthermore still endure today.

I wonder, as great Cold War actors from Henry Kissinger to the late Mikhail Gorbachev and Helmut Schmidt have already done, how such a degeneration of Russian–European relations was possible; with Moscow's unacceptable recourse to arms it signaled Russia's intention to divorce itself from the West.

However, the fact remains that the European Union has achieved its greatest results without the use of arms, but by putting its democratic standards into practice and exporting them through its aid programs. Despite the many well-argued criticisms made herein concerning that practice, in the long run those interventions have been decisive for many of the countries that are now full members of the European Union. The new categories of *Weaponization of Aid* and *Aidization of Weapons* that this book introduces to define the unprecedented model of *Interventionist Aid* tell the story of the historical turning point that took place before our eyes in the war in Ukraine. And that will affect the entire future of international relations.

While wars have been traumatic moments in which the balance of power is redefined on a global scale, it is nonetheless true that it is from the most solid and shared peace agreements that the most enduring world orders have emerged.

Expressing one's wishes both for an end to the war and that the competition between foreign policy interests be fought through aid wars instead of cannons is not a vain utopian exercise. Simply, it represents hope for the repetition of one of those returns to the future which, for better or worse, European history has accustomed us.

Professor Romano Prodi,
President of the European Commission (1999–2004)

1 Interventionist Aid

True Aid Revolution

According to the Office of the UN High Commissioner for Human Rights (OHCHR),[1] the number of civilian casualties in the first 14 months of the war in Ukraine amounted to almost 23,000 (around 8,500 dead and 14,300 wounded). Meanwhile, the World Health Organization (WHO) estimated more than 112,000 Ukrainian deaths from Covid-19, largely due to the population's lack of vaccination coverage.[2] Quantifying the death potential of a catastrophe is not only a sad exercise but also an impossible one, as such figures might be inaccurate: pandemic casualties were probably overestimated, while war casualties were certainly underestimated.

However, they point to another incontrovertible fact. In 2021, Kyiv's repeated and urgent requests to the West for vaccine doses were shrugged off by the same donors who less than a year later would rush to help the country "for the good of the Ukrainian people", i.e., after the Russian military invasion. It is natural to wonder why they reacted in such radically opposite ways to two historically close catastrophes which both brought death on a large scale beyond macabre quantification efforts; this is especially since, to further accentuate the difference with the pandemic scenario, the aid deployed in the outbreak of the Ukrainian war was unprecedented both in quantity and quality.

To justify this difference, it can be argued that in the exceptional Covid-19 pandemic, aid from Western donors was not possible because they themselves were plagued by a severe shortage of vaccine doses. It is a valid and objective argument that, however,

DOI: 10.4324/9781003382157-1

does not exclude but rather supports the hypothesis that the donors acted according to political considerations. First, there is the fact that the lack of vaccines in the West was by no means accidental, but rather the outcome of the choice of an Economic-Commercial Vaccine produced by Big Pharma, to the development of which portions of health sovereignty were ceded.

Moreover, the Ukrainian case was a perfect example of how so-called *Vaccine Diplomacy* systematically and overwhelmingly put political choices before humanitarian ones. Proof of this was Moscow's offer to provide Ukraine with sufficient doses of its state-owned vaccine Sputnik V free of charge. This aid was anything but disinterested and aimed to re-create a political bond to bring Kyiv back into the Russian orbit; this as, in 2014, Kyiv had switched to the Western front. Evidence that the decision being made was conditioned by political choices was also provided by the fact that Ukraine was initially in favor of accepting the Russian proposal. Subsequently, however – to avoid souring the relationship with its Western partners – the former aligned itself with the West's clear-cut closure towards the only vaccine that was available in sufficient quantities to deal with Ukraine's Covid-19 emergency at the beginning of 2021.

Finally, proof of the above was also found in Western opposition to the Russian vaccine for purely political reasons. This was demonstrated by the iconic case of the Republic of San Marino, a sovereign micro-state enclaved within Italy, which became the world's first Covid-free country thanks to Sputnik V; at that time Rome was, in reality, prolonging the pandemic crisis by its refusal to use the geo-political vaccine offered by Moscow.

Another argument for understanding the far stronger Western reaction at the outbreak of war in Ukraine frames it as a legitimate response given to Russia's blatant violation of one of the most sacred principles of international law, namely that no territorial change can be achieved by force. It is a valid argument that again reinforces the assumption of donor states who, in mobilizing in defence of the quintessential political principle of sovereignty, did not prioritize humanitarian considerations. It also indicates that – in the case of Ukraine – alongside international law, donors were also driven by geo-political considerations. For example, much less Western support was given to Tbilisi during the previous

Russian-Georgian conflict, though the latter was, in many aspects, similar to the Ukrainian crisis.

In other words, despite the severity of the impact on the population and the high number of casualties, the 2021 pandemic crisis in Ukraine did not provoke the same level of alarm in Western donors as the Russian military attack; this because the former represented neither a real geo-political risk (e.g. the return of Kyiv to the Russian sphere of influence) nor a dangerous precedent involving the violation of international law (e.g. the military invasion of a sovereign state).

Quite understandably, these considerations were absent from the official narratives of Western donors engaged in the age-old problem of translating foreign policy choices into mass communication form, to gain popular consent. As a result, while much has been said about aid at the outbreak of war in Ukraine, the aid policy revolution taking place in this very crisis went almost unnoticed.

For those who observe aid between states to decode international relations, this was a textbook case so exceptional that it seemed to be the result of a table-top simulation. More specifically, it clarified the present and past scenario of a conflict that, before the tanks, had long been fought by the same actors on the ground of aid.

But not only this.

At a general level, it saw astonishing innovations in the very manner in which inter-state aid itself is understood, communicated, and put into practice; it thus marked a historical, conceptual, and political turning point in its uninterrupted growth process that began at the end of World War II. At that moment in history aid became an emerging driver of relations between state actors at the international level. The protagonists increasingly conditioned one other geopolitically through new forms of assistance, rather than traditional instruments of war or trade.

Aid in the Ukrainian war left a mark beyond its specific context that was far stronger and more pronounced than aid in the Covid-19 crisis that immediately preceded it, despite the unparalleled global impact experienced during the immediate aftermath of the pandemic outbreak. The following work takes the above considerations as a starting point, to propose a political-institutional re-reading of the Ukrainian war crisis from the perspective of the inter-state aid policies that characterized it.

Following an uncommon approach to classic Foreign Aid narratives (usually they are focused more on the values inspiring the aid intervention, leaving aside eventual political-economic interests) it was decided to organize this work in a easy-to-read form, even and especially for non-specialists. For this reason, in Chapter 1 key findings and judgements are summarized in a more extended form than in the traditional introduction to a book.

The aid policies in the outbreak of the war in Ukraine were as relevant in a historical-political perspective as the war event itself. From the perspective of the History of International Relations, this surprise-war triggered by one country's (Russia's) invasion of a neighboring country (Ukraine), unfortunately featured nothing new; however, the inter-state aid that followed has been unprecedented in many ways. The echo it is bound to leave on the dynamics of the international system will go far beyond the individual Ukrainian case and the aid sector alone. This makes the conclusions of this work a useful element for those who deal with international relations *tout court*, either as a whole or from points of view that do not directly concern inter-state aid.

The approach followed herein is the one recently developed in our work "Re-Framing Foreign Aid History and Politics" (Routledge, 2022), which was completed two months before the outbreak of the war in Ukraine. In that text the aid provided, *inter alia,* during the Covid-19 crisis of 2020–2021 was framed in light of its high political significance. In seeing aid as a foreign policy instrument that primarily pursues the national interest of donor states, this approach focuses on the dynamics of power, political obligation, and competition that are established between donors and recipients. In other words, the institutional actors that give and receive aid at the international level.

This book is therefore intended to be an ideal continuation of the aforementioned work, extending the same interpretive key to the specific case of aid in the war in Ukraine, with a focus on the first 14 months following the outbreak of that conflict. To this end, the heart of its analysis revolves around two comparisons of aid in the Ukrainian scenario with, respectively, a historical case that is in many ways similar (aid at the outbreak of the war in Bosnia and Herzegovina (BiH) in 1992) and a case immediately preceding it (aid in the pandemic crisis in 2020–2021)

The first comparison is useful to define in detail the historical origins, political dynamics, and specific characteristics of aid in Ukraine which made it unique among wartime assistance scenarios. Despite the strong differences underlying the two crises, the elements that emerge from this comparison provide a frame of reference that allows us to proceed to the second comparison. This consists in capturing the common political aspects between aid provided during the Covid-19 and in the Ukrainian war. In turn, the comparison with the pandemic case frames the aspects that make the Ukrainian case a real revolution in the field of inter-state aid relations.

Key Conclusions and Findings of This Book

Key *Conclusions* emerged, which can be traced back to three sets of issues:

- Aid to Ukraine from 1991 to 2022 as historical early symptoms of the war;
- Eight technical and political peculiarities of inter-state aid in the Ukrainian war; and
- Political, conceptual, historical implications (and future forecasts) of the Ukrainian case.

The "Aid War" 1991–2021

Since its independence in 1991, Ukraine has been the recipient of aid programs by the same donors who faced off in the 2022 conflict. The period in between is an essential historical phase to understand the symptoms of today's crisis, as it anticipated the themes and directions of the clash between the West and Russia over Ukraine's geo-political location.

This 30-year period can be chronologically divided into four phases depending on the alternation of pro-Western or pro-Russian governments in Kyiv, that were decisive in defining the relations between the donors and their Ukrainian counterparts: (a) from 1991 to 2004; (b) from 2005 to 2010; (c) from 2010 to 2014; (d) from 2014 to 2022.

In the first phase which covers as much as half of the three decades of aid (until 2004), the West, in particular the EU, became politically disinterested in Ukraine. This effectively left Russia with almost unchallenged influence over the country. During this phase, Western aid (more interested in economic cooperation than in liberal-democratic development) coexisted with Russian aid; the latter, which was composed of the concession of natural and financial resources on very favorable terms.

In the period that followed (the second and third phases), aid was instead an expression of donors' geo-political competition to obtain and/or keep Ukraine within their sphere of influence. It represented an *Aid War* that peaked in 2014, when pro-Russian President Viktor Yanukovich openly preferred Russian financial aid to European aid, triggering the Maidan square uprising that led to his defenestration and flight to Russia. Together with the Russian annexation of Crimea, these two moments marked a breaking point in the country between pro-Western and pro-Russian political forces and their respective donors.

In the years leading up to the war, the West intensively supported the Kyiv government on the path of Atlantic military integration more than that of European political integration. Meanwhile Moscow provided increasing aid to the eastern regions in open confrontation with Kyiv, bearing the costs of what was already interpreted to be a *de facto* secession attempt from Ukraine.

Eight Peculiarities of Aid in the Ukrainian War

Comparison of the Ukrainian and Bosnian cases underline how the same bilateral donors, although driven by foreign policy interests, exhibited opposite types of reactions in two war scenarios featuring similar characteristics but very different geopolitical contexts. Long reluctant to intervene and put an end to a years-long massacre in BiH, both sets of donors decided to immediately intervene in Ukraine with unprecedented political determination and a very strong deployment of means. This gave Kyiv wide-ranging aid that was primarily military and financial in nature.

From the very first days of the outbreak of war, inter-state aid was characterized by at least eight peculiarities compared to what had commonly been seen at the start of similar war scenarios:

- *Response speed of Western Bilateral Donors.* Western Bilateral Donors immediately converged on the common strategy of sending wide-ranging aid to Ukraine.
- *Leading role and primacy of Western Bilateral Donors.* Western Bilateral Donors had a leading role in defining the overall political framework and technical content of aid, marginalizing non-governmental actors and multilateral agencies that are generally active in conflict scenarios. As a result, the official priority objective of Western aid, to which all others were subordinated, was to repel the invasion by the Russian military.
- *The Recipient Partner.* Aid had a single institutional recipient (the Ukrainian government) which was treated as an equal partner to the Donors and was highly involved in decision making and in co-defining and co-managing all Western assistance to Kyiv.
- *Quantity and diversification of aid.* There has been an enormous quantity of diversified aid concentrated mostly on new areas of intervention (financial, political-institutional, military), relegating traditional humanitarian aid to second place.
- *Aid turned into a hybrid weapon.* Russia turned access to essential goods that was traditionally at the center of its aid policies (first and foremost in the energy and agri-food sectors) into a tactical instrument of pressure and a leading hybrid weapon to be used globally, depending on the course of the war.
- *Weapons as primary aid.* Donors have legitimized the provision of military assistance in an ongoing conflict as if it was a first aid priority, openly making the supply of armaments the main item of expenditure of Western assistance to Ukraine.
- *Premature opening of the post-conflict phase.* In the name of political support for Ukraine, Western donors anticipated unusual decisions for a war context in its early stages, such as (a) the acceleration of Kyiv's entry process to the EU and (b) the formal opening of a preparatory phase for Ukraine's post-war reconstruction.
- *Sanctions as aid.* The coordinated and integrated use of Sanctions and Aid in a manner that changes the occasional use thereof to systematic recourse, with aims tied to tactical warfare.

This has taken place with an unprecedented level of involvement of the Ukrainian side in the definition of this use. In this context sanctions were a weapon of war (against the enemy) and a source of aid (for the *Recipient Partner*).

Political, Conceptual, Historical (and Future) Implications

Aid in the Ukrainian war brought about a radical conceptual, political, and historical shift in the evolution of inter-state aid, outlining some hypotheses of related future scenarios.

The Political Dimension: Interventionist Aid

The Ukrainian case defined and put into practice a new unstructured model of *Interventionist Aid*, made up of new practices ideally replicable in other contexts, that:

(a) Aimed to influence the outcome of the crisis in which it operated, i.e., was set up as *Success-Oriented Aid* determined to achieve strategic objectives to orient the course of events in the intervention scenario;
(b) Openly placed tactical aims before humanitarian ones, with interventions entailing assistance in the most diverse sectors, starting with the military and financial ones; the aforesaid were provided in the course of an ongoing conflict; and
(c) Involved protagonists that were Western Bilateral Donors active directly in the field in unmediated coordination with a single governmental recipient in Kyiv who, on the strength of its equal partnership status, influenced the programming, composition, and management of aid in an ex-ante and ex-post manner. Instances of *Recipient-Driven Aid* were frequently seen in this context.

The Conceptual Dimension: Anarchical Aid as a Key Component of War

Interventionist Aid confirmed and indeed reinforced a realist theoretical approach whereby international aid used by state actors for their foreign policy objectives is best defined by the concept of "International Aid Public Policies (IAPPs)", in preference to "Foreign Aid", given that the former focuses on the political dynamics between institutional donors and recipients at bilateral and multilateral levels, as well as the impact of inter-state aid on international relations.

Three conceptual spin-offs have derived from IAPP practices since the outbreak of the Ukrainian war:

(a) *Weaponization of Aid*: defined as the systematic transformation by Russia of classic aid goods and assets into hybrid weapons;
(b) *Aidization of Weapons*: defined as the political and financial prioritization by Western Bilateral Donors of a wide range of military aid during the outbreak of a war;
(c) *Anarchical Aid as a Key Component of War*: Interventionist Aid, through such new and unregulated practices of *Weaponization* and *Aidization*, has been turned into a necessary, key – and yet anarchical – aid component in an ongoing conflict.

The Historical Dimension: The "Interventionist Aid" Phase

In the historical evolution of IAPPs, the Ukrainian Interventionist Aid marked a turning point that completed and concluded changes initiated in the previous two years by aid provided during Covid-19.

Combined, Interventionist Aid and Pandemic Aid contributed to the overcoming of the historical Transition Aid Phase that had characterized the post-Cold War following the fall of the Berlin Wall. At the same time, they marked the beginning of a new historical "Interventionist Aid Phase" that was made up of wide-ranging multi-sector aid used to actively influence the course of events in the scenario of action, including traditional wars. Thus, putting tactical objectives before the humanitarian or emergency objectives of classic Foreign Aid in a warfare context.

New World Order and Interventionist Aid

The opening of the new Interventionist Aid Phase would go hand in hand with the redefinition of the international balance of powers which has been accelerated by the war in Ukraine. If this is consolidated, interventionism would become part of the building blocks of a new world order, characterized by an increase in the global importance of broad-based state aid policies, set to act directly in scenarios of geopolitical importance, and ideally not limited to emergency crises. This would mark the normalization of tactical bilateral aid to achieve primary political objectives that are openly granted precedence to humanitarian ones; meanwhile multilateral donors would further reduce their role and international operations.

Post-Democracy Aid

The second projection on the future impact of Interventionist Aid sketches a possible worsening of the consensus crisis in institutional communications concerning aid that has been ongoing for some time and was exacerbated during the pandemic and the Ukrainian war. Although radical changes in aid policies have taken place, the related institutional narratives have remained anchored in the old emotional categories of "Good Foreign Aid". Future systematic reliance on Interventionist Aid would re-propose a widening of the gap between politics and civil society, not so much because of its actions but due to the inability of traditional aid narratives to frame it credibly whilst avoiding the contradictions of the new approach compared to the neutralist aid of the past.

Like health, welfare and labor policies, aid policies would enter the realm of political confrontation, removing them from the category of topics exempted from criticism which they have long belonged to. Greater scrutiny of Interventionist Aid and its narratives would reinforce a critical view of inter-state aid, leading growing sectors of the public to perceive it as something imposed from above, regardless of popular will. A widespread perception in the public opinion on so-called Post-Democracy Aid policies will be a particular concern for Western donor states, grappling with the constant and difficult challenge of reaching coherence between the political realism of Interventionist Aid and their liberal-democratic system of values and constitutional principles.

War World Aid

Finally, a new world order based on Interventionist Aid would mark a definitive shift from the non-military Aid Wars fought by donor states in the post-Cold War towards a future in which aid will be used to fuel real military confrontations by proxy. A global scenario of World War Aid would emerge, with a multiplicity of circumscribed regional conflicts spread over major scenarios; this would see conflicts fought remotely and informally by donors using aid supplemented by sanctions. In this scenario international relations would regress to nineteenth-century-style patchwork conflicts, challenging the basic parameters of human, political and social rights achieved since the end of the Cold War. Meanwhile, Europe's international relevance would enter a long recessionary phase, with geopolitical axes polarizing westward towards the United States and eastward towards a Chinese-driven Greater Eurasia. In a paradoxical fashion, the new world order would feature clear and well-defined opposing camps; this after decades of World Disorder, with unclear zones of influence characterized by the presence of unstable yet long-term balances of power and non-military Aid Wars. The resultant scenario would be traversed by more widespread, low-intensity hybrid conflicts, fought with Interventionist Aid practices and objectives.

Ex-Ante Disclaimer: The Sense of This Book

The introduction to our previous book, cited above, concluded with some clarification on the sense one should (not) attribute to the main conclusions presented therein. Dealing with a subject that pulled at one's heartstrings, we urged readers not to adopt prejudicial negative judgements when faced with the descriptive analyses that reported critical aspects of specific case studies on the use of aid in international relations *tout court*. This caveat must be reiterated (and even supplemented) here, even more so at the beginning of a new book that arose from the intersection of the delicate issue of inter-state aid with the very sensitive issue of war while the conflict in Ukraine is still ongoing.

Much of this book focuses on the new model of Interventionist Aid that has emerged during the war in Ukraine, overshadowing the traditional forms of humanitarian aid used in the past, i.e., in other emergency war scenarios. The peculiarities of Interventionist Aid described here, together with the technical and political issues raised by the discussion of these peculiarities, inevitably portray it as a hyper-realist regression, or a step backwards from a traditional positive depiction of Foreign Aid as "Good Aid" as it is aimed primarily at development and humanitarian targets.

The critical analyses proposed here must be read keeping in mind some fundamental clarification:

(1) Interventionist Aid was not the cause but the effect of the war in Ukraine, which effectively put the nail in the coffin of classic "Good" Foreign Aid modalities. Despite having served as a foreign policy tool, the latter had for decades succeeded in keeping competition between donor states on non-military grounds.

(2) The main objective of this work is to identify and describe as many peculiarities of Interventionist Aid as possible and contextualize them within the historical, political, and conceptual process in which the evolution of aid is defined in international relations. Given that the theoretical approach adopted herein belongs to the realist tradition, another aim of this work is to show that donor states have primarily used aid to put their foreign policy objectives into practice. This should in no way be read as a criticism of determination to assist Kyiv before and after the invasion.

(3) Interventionist Aid did not have a common direction and shared practices but was the result of practices introduced in a scattered and opposing order, so that its two main constituent elements were the Russian Weaponization of Aid (raw materials and natural resources used as hybrid weapons) and the Western Aidization of Weapons (prioritization of wide-ranging military assistance given to Kyiv).

(4) This work addresses the problems with much of Western aid simply because Russia, by invading Ukraine militarily, has, in fact, blatantly abdicated its status of Re-emerging Donor; ironically that was a role in which it had invested so much over the previous two decades. This is the only reason why it is the incongruities in the Western aid system and its narratives that are mainly observed here; some of those anomalies are serious and had manifested themselves well before the conflict. Pointing out the aforesaid is in no way – directly or indirectly – intended to constitute justification or acceptance of the war in Ukraine. As pointed out in the conclusion of our previous book, although our research is on the political interests of

donors and the frequent inconsistencies of international aid policies, if one had to choose, it would still be better for a recipient country to be invaded by aid rather than tanks.

The misfortune of having lived through and the luck of having survived a real war in Bosnia and Herzegovina in his youth led the Author of these pages to develop a feeling of serious annoyance towards all armed conflicts, without exception. It is a natural, empathetic feeling that borders on physical pain; this sentiment has little in common with a certain militant brand of pacifism which could be looked upon with suspicion both for its political matrix as well as its utopian tendencies as an end onto themselves.

While this work was inspired by the intention to cover the topics herein in as analytical and objective a manner as possible, dedicating it to all civilian victims of military conflicts best expresses the Author's personal and unconditional rejection of war.

Notes

1 See www.ohchr.org/en/news/2023/05/ukraine-civilian-casualty-update-8-may-2023#:~:text=From%201%20to%207%20May%202023%2C%20OHCHR%20recorded%20221%20civilian,sex%20is%20not%20yet%20known.
2 See https://covid19.who.int.

2 Aid Connecting Virus and War

Aid, a Mainstream Word

The outbreak of Covid-19 (February 2020) and the Russian-Ukrainian conflict only two years later (February 2022) with the pandemic still in progress have created a dual-crisis scenario unprecedented in recent history (Fidler, 2020: 1309–1312; Chohan, 2021; Pellicciari, 2022b: 61–77). Coming as a surprise, at least in the way they unfolded, these crises have overlapped, magnifying the joint impact of their effects and consequences.

Easy comparisons have been produced in the search for links between two traumatic world occurrences which took place in such rapid succession. Such theories have been concocted in an attempt to assign an overarching "meaning" to these events, i.e., to make them easier to deal with, in the name of a single common spirit of resistance. Lumping war and a virus together was an understandable reaction; this association was facilitated by the ease with which many leaders in 2020 made extensive use of the war analogy to describe the outbreak of the pandemic and justify the introduction of exceptional measures restricting personal freedom to contain the number of contagions (Malchrzak et al., 2022; Dhawan, Choudhary and Saied, 2022). After declaring "war on Covid-19" for many months during the lockdown, and then later during the vaccination campaigns, when a real war broke out in Ukraine and the WHO had not yet decreed the end of the pandemic, it came naturally to adopt the same attitude towards the two events.

The normal tendency to relate them, however, soon led to journalistic excesses and exaggerations in seeking and even emphasizing similarities between two crises that were actually very

DOI: 10.4324/9781003382157-2

different. Starting from the very nature of the factors that triggered them and the scenarios they generated. When it appeared, the pandemic simultaneously confronted all world governments without distinction with the prospect of the same natural disaster, posing the same type of problems and emergencies for the first time. Opposing an unknown virus has effectively suspended – and thus reduced – the level of conflict and opposition in the international system. Faced with the freezing of clashes in the various open theatres of confrontation, some observers even predicted the preconditions for the materialization of a reset moment and a positive "re-globalization" movement (Pellicciari, 2021).

The outbreak of war in Ukraine, on the contrary, was a crisis having purely human origins and was detonated by the use of the tragic but far-from-new method of the military invasion of a country by its neighbor. Such a genesis of the crisis has increased immediate instability in international relations as well as the level of conflict in the pre-existing so-called World Disorder (Gehring, 2022; Mbah and Wasum, 2022: 144–53). Notwithstanding these structural differences, it is nevertheless true that there are aspects that concerned both Covid-19 and the war in Ukraine that deserve further investigation. This is so precisely to provide understanding of any real level of connection between the two events that goes beyond an emotional depiction of their causal connection influenced by a determinist view of history.

One of the main visible phenomena common to the two crises has been the frequency of use of the term *aid*, which was among the most recurrent words during the pandemic and the conflict in Ukraine, after the terms *virus* and *war*, respectively. Concerning the pandemic, a spontaneous orientation towards aid (given and requested) in the face of a health emergency equally looming over the whole of humanity was predictable and natural. This was the ideal terrain for the spread of a wide and transversal sense of solidarity (Kobayashi, Heinrich and Bryant, 2021). Less obvious was the prominence of aid at the outbreak of the war in Ukraine, as this was a context of open military opposition that was – by definition – less naturally inclined to favor international cooperation (Ibid.).

According to a predictable dynamic, the pandemic and the war have created unexpected and multiple situations of sudden need and naturally laid the prerequisite bases for the organization of initiatives to alleviate them, albeit animated by a different spirit (Trebesch et al., 2023; Szőke and Kolos, 2023; Grossi and Vakulenko, 2023; Bosse, 2022: 531–546; Dräger, Gründler and Potrafke, 2022; Mills, 2022; Hashimova, 2022). The term has spread quite widely, and been involved in radically different contexts and actions, reflecting its extreme versatility and transversality of use. It has also confirmed well-known ambiguities, being able to host multiple contents, some of which are diametrically opposed. In the age of social media and continuous flow of unverified information, due to the ease with which it can be used and the immediacy of understanding it inspires, the term *aid* has become a key mainstream word in two of the major international crises in the current century.

Contributing to the unconditional and generic use of the term was the *horror vacui*-based need of content-hungry infotainment to fill 24-hour broadcasting spaces, whose primary objective is gaining an audience rather than providing information and analysis. In the constant search for iconic symbols to feed a continuous flow of news, *aid* in its broadest sense has been a functional term for the construction of narratives primarily aimed at stimulating emotions and/or obtaining consensus. This resulted in the reintroduction of a vague idea of aid that has inserted initiatives that were only generically self-declared "assistance actions" in their respective area of intervention. In the media that have reported on the pandemic and war crises, it has been normal to place under the banner of aid interventions that were, in reality, heterogeneous in nature, in terms of the type of actors involved and the assistance provided. This has resulted in an indiscriminate association of humanitarian aid with military assistance, energy supply with health aid, and extra-ordinary incentives for the recovery of domestic economies with traditional types of Foreign Aid development interventions (Morgenthau, 1962; Furia, 2015; Hall, 2006; Wight; 1978).

The emergence of *aid* as a mainstream keyword in a crisis-filled era has led to a disregard for the distinctive features of individual aid initiatives, fueling old ambiguities surrounding the meaning of the term. Indeed, it has been used to promote rhetorical messages instead of analyses of facts, and the distinction between the public or private matrix of aid is among the aspects most systematically neglected. The narratives of infotainment have equated structured state-funded aid policies with those of non-governmental sector aid. The latter were more fragmented and oriented towards addressing the basic needs created by Covid-19 and war. Similarly, among the numerous appeals for aid addressed to the European Commission during the pandemic, it was not clear whether these came from EU Member States or non-EU countries: just as it was often not clear, among the various appeals for aid addressed to central governments, whether they originated from local territorial authorities or professional associations. As far as non-governmental aid is concerned, it has proved to be a *mare magnum* principally made up of many small-scale actors, who act independently mainly in the humanitarian field (Trebesch et al., 2023; Bosse, 2022; Szőke and Kolos, 2023; Grossi and Vakulenko, 2023; Dräger, Gründler and Potrafke, 2022; Pishchikova, 2010; Woehrel, 2014).

While in the case of Covid-19 non-governmental aid moved on the terrain of popular fund-raising and basic healthcare given to specific, vulnerable categories infected by the virus, in the case of the Ukrainian conflict it has returned to dealing with types of intervention typical of the non-governmental tradition: organizing emergency humanitarian aid for categories of war victims, starting from refugees and displaced persons (Brezhneva and Ukhova, 2013; Hill, 2011; Pickering, 2014: 31–43; Gilbert, 2016: 717–29; Gray, 2015: 273–88). Praiseworthy in its intentions, often much less so in its effectiveness, non-governmental aid has typically been responsible for rather limited interventions compared to the symbolic scope and visibility it has achieved in the media (Pishchikova, 2010; Woehrel, 2014). Rather than on the concrete amount of aid moved, which has remained limited overall, it has contributed to raising public awareness of the seriousness of the consequences of crises, helping to give a first-hand view of their development on the ground.

However, non-governmental aid as a whole proved to be a difficult subject to study, precisely because of its compartmentalized nature composed of autonomous monads, often too small to be fully analyzed. The widespread difficulty in finding reliable, homogeneous and accessible data on specific assistance initiatives, particularly those by smaller actors, makes it difficult to reconstruct the overall picture of private aid and its underlying dynamics (Trebesch et al., 2023; Bosse, 2022; Pishchikova, 2010; Woehrel, 2014).

It is no coincidence that research and publications on aid issued by the non-governmental sector heavily lean towards apologetically observing the objectives pursued and the value system that donors claim to be inspired by, while remaining deficient in terms of reporting the real impact of interventions (Pellicciari, 2017; 2022a; Furia, 2015). An accomplice to communications aimed at fundraising is the narrative of what the aid promised to do; this increasingly receives more space than the objective reporting of what has already been accomplished. Each private donor's assistance intervention is a story onto itself and is jealously represented as a self-standing experience, making a comprehensive analysis of the aid initiatives very difficult. Therefore, for the purposes of this work, the interventions of the non-governmental sector are not a reliable perspective from which to identify any eventual overlap of political points between aid in the war in Ukraine and in the pandemic.

International Aid Public Policies to Compare Pandemic and War

The opposite argument concerns international aid originating from the public sector, which constitutes an excellent indicator for a political-institutional analysis comparing the context of two different crises. Unlike aid from the private sector, which is difficult to categorize because it is organized in an *ad hoc* manner, public-sector aid is better defined, better structured, institutionalized, and continuous. Furthermore, being documented and traceable makes it less insidious as a direct object of study and being defined by verifiable indicators renders it a more precise systemic reference.

Thus, herein the cases of the Ukrainian war and pandemic are compared from the perspective of the public aid that characterized them, to highlight the common aspects they share notwithstanding the profoundly different nature of the crises involved. The latter is challenging, as both cases were marked by the prominent role played by state-funded aid, particularly at the international level (Trebesch et al., 2023; Szőke and Kolos, 2023; Grossi and Vakulenko, 2023; Bosse, 2022; Dräger, Gründler and Potrafke, 2022; Hashimova, 2022). From the onset of the two crises, in fact, donor states that were active directly on the ground appeared on the scene. Likewise, international relations were almost entirely channeled at the level of inter-state aid.

During the pandemic, the latter initially focused on medical supplies for protection and prophylaxis against contagion; the aims thereof subsequently shifted, largely towards those expressed herein by the term *Vaccine Diplomacy*. In the case of the outbreak of the Ukrainian war, it largely concerned the broad spectrum of aid that Western countries sent to Kyiv to oppose the Russian military invasion. To facilitate a direct comparison between the inter-state aid in the Ukrainian war and in the pandemic, we will adopt an approach that considers state-funded aid in the international dimension to be a primary expression of the donor's foreign policy.

As such, aid has a strong impact on international relations at the bilateral and multilateral level. In treating aid as a new driver of inter-state relations alternative to the classic channels of war and trade, this approach views inter-state aid policies from an integrated historical, conceptual and political perspective. This is done by fitting aid into the general framework of realist thinking in international relations, i.e., namely drawing up the classical origins of this school of thought in Niccolò Machiavelli and Thomas Hobbes. Furthermore, included in this thread are the realist variations that developed during World War II and the Cold War (Carr, 1939; Wight, 1946; Kennan, 1947; Morgenthau, 1962; 1978; Huntington, 1970; Waltz, 1978), up to its more contemporary evolutions (Kissinger, 2014).

The assumption is that donor states use aid to power politics in defense of their national interests, in such a way as to achieve political benefits that are, overall, greater than those enjoyed by the recipient states. The result is an analysis less interested in observing aid intervention as such, and rather more intent on the dynamics of political obligation that are established between donors and recipients. In turn, consistent focus remains on the competition among donors themselves, to gain primacy of action in areas hosting their geo-political interests.

In pursuit of the implications and political dynamics of inter-state aid, this approach has been complemented by the introduction of a new concept of *International Aid Public Policy* (hereafter IAPP) that goes beyond classic *Foreign Aid* because it (a) focuses on the foreign policy interests that drive donor states and the dynamics of their relationship with recipient states; and

(b) considers aid any transaction carried out on favorable terms between donor states and recipient states, regardless of the area of assistance and whether it is formally labelled as Foreign Aid (Pellicciari, 2022a; 2017).

Applied recently to the analysis of a series of historical cases, including aid during the main Covid-19 phases (Ibid.), this realist theoretical approach has confirmed its validity in identifying the political aspects of *Pandemic Aid,* concluding that:

- inter-state aid during the pandemic was part of the uninterrupted historical growth process of IAPPs that began after the end of World War II;
- interventions during the emergency phase of the pandemic, especially in the subsequent clash of *Vaccine Diplomacy*, have shown how aid has catalyzed and influenced many behaviors in international relations and had a central impact on shaping its balance of powers (Fidler, 2020; Chohan, 2021);
- bilateral donors used health aid while primarily following geopolitical logic and in evident defense of their national interests;
- in the first emergency phase, donor states competed over the procurement and supply of medical supplies to limit the spread of the virus;
- the following phase was dominated by *Vaccine Diplomacy*, with an open confrontation between a privately produced *Economic-Commercial Vaccine* model that limited the state aid policies of Western countries and a purely public Eastern *Geo-political Vaccine* used as a foreign policy tool by Russia and China (Pellicciari, 2022a).

Framing Aid in the Ukrainian War

Taking as a given the results of the above analysis of *Pandemic Aid*, a large part of this work is dedicated to applying the same realist approach of the IAPP concept to the Ukrainian war case. The aim is to identify in detail the concrete elements and specific features that have made aid in the Ukrainian conflict unprecedented, as well as contextualize them within the historical process of growth and evolution of IAPPs. Starting from the search for common aspects with aid in the pandemic crisis.

In this regard, the work is divided into six sections, each of which offers an analysis that is to be conceived as part of the overall framing of aid (intended as IAPP) in the Ukrainian War:

(1) *Historical analysis of aid to Ukraine from 1991 to 2021.* Precisely in virtue of a vision that considers IAPPs crucial in the evolution of international relations, this work starts from a historical reconstruction of the inter-state aid received by Kyiv after its independence in 1991. Looking for historical early symptoms of the 2022 war is a central aspect, above all in a Ukrainian context, given its very high level of exposure and permeability to international aid. The aforesaid period constituted three decades that anticipated themes and dynamics of the geo-political dispute over the country's future, and in which aid became the first area of confrontation between many of the actors who would later become the protagonists of the war scenario.

(2) *Comparison of the Ukrainian context in 2022 and the Bosnian context in 1992.* The comparison of two European war outbreaks involving the same donors thirty years apart allows us to identify the main political and technical peculiarities of aid in Ukraine. A picture of clear differences emerges between the two cases, both in terms of the characteristics of the respective domestic and international contexts and in terms of the *modus operandi* of the donors; in Ukraine, *de facto*, they defined and put into practice a new model of *Interventionist Aid* as opposed to the *Neutralist Aid* that had characterized the Bosnian case.

(3) *Analysis of the peculiarities of Interventionist Aid.* As the focus of this work is primarily on framing aid in the Ukrainian case, each of the eight peculiarities of Ukrainian Interventionist Aid are described individually, focusing on the main aspects of innovation and change represented therein. Given the strategic focus and political significance they have assigned to Interventionist Aid, we will also indicate the main issues raised for each of the eight peculiarities.

(4) *Comparison between Ukrainian Interventionist Aid and Pandemic Aid.* Having scrutinized the characteristics of aid in the war in Ukraine, the contextual frame is complete for

one of the initial objectives of this work: a comparison with *Pandemic Aid*. Although more similarities than differences exist between the two, Interventionist Aid possesses a superior degree of innovation, albeit an unregulated one, that marks a major turning point in IAPPs.

(5) *The implications of Interventionist Aid in the evolution of IAPPs*. The final historical analysis will contextualize aid in the war in Ukraine in the evolutionary process of IAPPs. Having identified the historical early symptoms, the peculiarities, and the structural innovations of Interventionist Aid, the analysis herein founds its main implications on the political, conceptual, and historical dimension of the IAPPs of the last decades. Specifically, we will examine this as consolidated during the post-Cold War phase following the collapse of the Berlin Wall.

(6) *The future of Interventionist Aid*. Presented here as a *postscript*, to mark their separation from the historical analysis, this work concludes with some predictions about a future new world order based on the systematic use of Interventionist Aid, forecasting two unpredictable developments. At the domestic level, a growing crisis is predicted concerning the legitimacy of Interventionist Aid, i.e., the perception of it as a post-democratic phenomenon, while at the international level a slide toward a World War Aid scenario is forecasted, i.e., one globally fought with Interventionist IAPPs on a broad spectrum, and moreover within major scenarios of geo-political relevance.

3 Ukrainian War Symptoms in Aid History

Aid to Ukraine (1991–2022)

From the perspective of inter-state aid policies, the first domestic and international symptoms of the Ukrainian crisis date back to three decades before the 2022 war, namely, to the time of the sudden and unexpected dissolution of the USSR (Radeljić, 2012; Craven, 1995: 333–413).

In the turbulent early 1990s, while in the Western Balkans new sovereignties arose due to a traumatic breakaway from the former Yugoslavia, the Soviet Socialist Republic of Ukraine achieved independence without encountering any significant obstacles. Indeed, it was almost encouraged in that process and even maintained its original internal federal borders from the Soviet period (Minakov et al., 2021; Kubicek, 2008; Subtelny, 2009). As in other post-Soviet contexts, the country faced the challenge of strengthening and modernizing its political-institutional structure, in line with the principles of the rule of law and free markets so typical of the liberal-democratic tradition embraced by former Soviet republics in reaction to the abjuration of communism.

Here, as elsewhere, the track record of reforms often remained well below the minimum standards set by Western donors in their transition assistance programs. However, over the decades, a process of institutionalization of the state developed which was manifested externally as the internationally recognized sovereignty of the country. Nevertheless, weighing on the domestic situation was an issue that, over time, has acquired strong international relevance, involving the difficult balancing act between the centre in Kyiv and the peripheries in the west and east of the country,

DOI: 10.4324/9781003382157-3

i.e., with Ukrainian and Russian linguistic majorities, respectively (Ibid.).

Unlike in the Western Balkans, the contrast here was not so much an ethnic matrix as one marked by historical-cultural differences rooted in orientations more open to Europe or more inclined towards Russia. In the decades before the war, the continuous intersection of these two options, featuring contrasts between the centre-periphery and regional East-West interests, has led Kyiv to alternate between radically opposed governments and foreign policies of either a pro-European (and, in time, Atlanticist), or a pro-Russian orientation (Minakov et al., 2021; Subtelny, 2009; Kubicek, 2008).

With the new century, the confrontation between these two orientations has gone beyond national borders and led to increasingly direct involvement in Ukrainian affairs by the Western bilateral and multilateral actors who have clashed with Russia. During the 1990s the latter continued to maintain an endemic link with the country, particularly with the leadership at the summit in Kyiv (Ibid.). At the same time, the competition between the two sides to extend, or maintain, their influence over a country of strategic importance in natural resource terms and, above all, geo-political location, has contributed to internationalizing and polarizing the internal opposition between pro-Russian and pro-Western options.

The central fact is that, in the decades leading up to the outbreak of war, the clash between the West and Russia to bring Ukraine into their sphere of influence took place on the terrain of their respective aid programs with the country. Until 2014 the donors' competition focused on the same recipient, i.e., the central government in Kyiv. The context changed dramatically after that period with the street defenestration of pro-Russian President Viktor Yanukovych by the pro-Western camp and the formal annexation of Crimea to the territory of the Russian Federation by Moscow (Kudelia, 2014; Mearsheimer, 2014). These two episodes could not be reconciled within the domestic political-institutional framework; indeed they created a rift between the central government in Kyiv supported by Western donors and the eastern area of the Donbas, i.e., the recipient of Russian aid. The result fuelled regional tension that degenerated into creeping internal guerrilla warfare.

From the perspective of inter-state aid, the Ukrainian case has stood out given the substantial assistance programs targeting Kyiv in the long period between its independence in 1991 and the outbreak of the war in 2022 (Milner in Hawkins et al., 2006; Trebesch et al., 2023; Hashimova, 2022). This was completely absent in the Western Balkans in the 1990s, which were affected by conflicts in conjunction with the declaration of independence of the new sovereignties that arose from the former Yugoslavia. They had not experienced direct foreign aid previous to that period.

Ukraine's long history as a recipient of Western and Russian assistance has influenced some of the peculiarities in the aid rendered during the outbreak of the war described below; these were almost never featured in the daily chronicles reporting on the 2022 conflict as if the area featured no past history (Trebesch et al., 2023; Hashimova, 2022).

This timespan can be divided into four phases, in a periodization pattern that in reality follows Kyiv's alternation between putative pro-Western and pro-Russian governments; this fluctuation was itself decisive in defining relations between the donors and their Ukrainian counterparts.

1991–2004	*The Aid without Reforms Phase*
2005–2010	*The Pro-European Ambition Phase*
2010–2014	*The War of Aid Phase*
2014–2022	*The Atlanticist Strategy Phase*

Tracing the broad outlines of this timespan suggests some conclusions that are crucial to understanding not only the main issues concerning aid to the country, but the whole context preparing for war; namely:

(a) the competition between Western donors and Russia over aid began long before the outbreak of the war and partially anticipated its themes; similarly, it prepared the ground for the conflict. All major contenders in the 2022 war have been among Ukraine's major donors since its independence in 1991;
(b) in the first half of the three decades of aid before the war, the West and in particular the EU were disinterested in Ukraine's democratic transition, instead concentrating aid on economic cooperation. This behavior left Russia free to exert nearly

uncontested political influence over the country in the first 15 years of its independence;
(c) The realistic prospect of European integration gained new momentum during the so-called first Orange Revolution in 2004, and yet until 2022 it was politically slowed down by the EU. The latter was dissatisfied with Kyiv's slowness in adopting the European standards required of EU candidate countries. Conversely, particularly after the 2014 Maidan revolution, the prospect of Kyiv's integration into the Atlantic Alliance became a reality. This was at the initiative of the US and NATO;
(d) since Ukraine's independence, Russia has mainly played its donor role through supplying Kyiv with raw materials and energy resources sold on favorable terms. This allowed Moscow to continue to exercise its role as a key donor, even during the turbulent 1990s of Russia's post-Soviet transition.

1991–2004 Aid without Reform

Excluding the initial two-and-a-half-year interlude of the first President Leonid Kravchuk, who pursued a rather amorphous, short-sighted, and self-absorbed policy (later erroneously characterized as pro-Western) and who neither ruled out nor meaningfully pursued stronger alliances with the US and the EU, the period in question coincided with the two presidential terms of Leonid Kuchma. The political term of the latter was the closest thing to a true political-system ruler that Ukraine had at the time (Minakov et al., 2021, Subtelny, 2009; Kubicek, 2008, Odey and Samuel, 2022). Of the 15 sovereign states that have emerged since the end of the USSR, Ukraine was, after Russia, the most politically important country of that lineup, and among the natural recipients of Western aid for the Post-Soviet region.

In general, the period in question saw the beginning of cooperation with Western partners that gradually became more active and coexisted with the old ties with Russia that the country inherited from the USSR. Grappling with a difficult economic situation (with hyperinflation reaching 10256% by 1993), endemic corruption, and widespread levels of organized crime, Ukraine demonstrated that it first had to organize and unify its economy. This, before it could develop a reasonable capacity to align its domestic and foreign policies with – or absorb assistance from – Western donors.

On their part, the main providers of aid (including, as time has shown, Russia) did not possess in-depth knowledge of the country or of the root causes of its persistent problems. Moreover, most strategy documents between Ukraine and aid providers were rather generic and feeble in design, with weak conditionalities and inconsistent mechanisms to monitor aid implementation. A comparison of today's agreements between the EU and Ukraine with those adopted in the 1990s highlights how the first agreements focused on areas that mainly affected neighboring countries and the region in general; they failed to aim for deep and comprehensive changes in Ukraine. As a result, among the elements of aid provided, no major programs tailored exclusively to Kyiv were present, i.e., measures that addressed political-institutional aspects to support the country in coping with its specific, dual post-Soviet and post-independence transition. Rather, types of assistance that suffered from the general Western approach to the Post-Soviet region in the 1990s were automatically applied in search of economic opportunities, natural resources, and new markets; those donors were effectively disinterested in promoting the country's political-institutional development (Pellicciari, 2022a; Wolczuk, 2004: 1–22).

Apart from specific initiatives in the strategic sector of denuclearization (an issue that also interested Russia at the time) Western aid was mainly focused on promoting the *Free Market Economy* rather than the *Rule of Law*. The trend started with initial, basic legislative regulation for a select few and fundamental institutions; it subsequently spread to small initiatives concerning human rights in the non-governmental sector. The result was a paradox whereby aid took place parallel to Ukrainian political life and without affecting (and often suffering from) widespread practices featuring authoritarianism, the arbitrary management of laws and power, endemic corruption, and the systematic private use of public resources. The Ukrainian leadership accepted this aid because it posed no risk to the internal *status quo* and fit into its policies of unbridled economic monopolization; meanwhile, foot-dragging occurred on democratic political organization, and inaction was witnessed on national security. Simultaneously, national unification sentiments crept into the educational and cultural sectors. All the while, the donors themselves were only superficially interested in Ukraine's democratic transition. Accordingly, the country was long treated as being destined to remain indefinitely outside the

European geo-political space (Minakov et al., 2021; Kubicek, 2005; De Ploeg, 2017; Subtelny, 2009, Wolczuk, 2004).

Exemplary in this respect is the total amount of aid received from the European Union, which was financially anything but minor, amounting as it did to some €4.2 billion[1] in the period from 1991 to 1999. The aforesaid figure included €2.8 billion in the five-year period between 1991 and 1995 (of which 1,215 billion European Currency Units (ECU) came from EU sources and the rest from the member states). Moreover, slightly over €1 billion in aid was contributed from 1998 to 2004.[2] Against these large sums, the actions in support of Ukraine's transition were made under the auspices of the general TACIS program, which was aimed at all former USSR countries. Initiated in 1991, TACIS technical assistance projects were provided for the duration of the 1990s in the form of fragmented and disconnected actions that generally were neither very relevant nor sustainable. A more defined framework for interventions was provided by the *Partnership and Cooperation Agreement*[3] (PCA, an almost standard omnibus agreement that established areas of bilateral cooperation between the EU and post-Soviet countries). Ukraine signed a PCA in 1994; however, the agreement did not enter into force until 1998 (Ibid.).

It was not until 2000 that cooperation between Ukraine and the EU became "dialogue-oriented",[4] with the European Council's adoption of the Regulation (No. 99/2000) on cooperation between the EU and the TACIS partner countries. The follow-up document, the *EU Action Plan on Justice and Home Affairs in Ukraine*,[5] which was approved by the EU Council on December 10, 2001, became the first substantial framework document to identify political cooperation priorities, starting from the country's crucial justice sector. Among other goals, it focused on the establishment of an independent and competent judiciary by targeting court system reform, the prevention of corruption, the development of the Unified Register of Court Decisions, and reform of the penitentiary system. The plan succeeded in producing successful but isolated cases through the internalization of the jurisprudence of the European Court of Human Rights as a source of law for Ukrainian courts. Moreover, the institutionalization of a comprehensive register of court decisions and, to a lesser extent, judicial reviews in specialized administrative courts were carried out. In practice, however, the overall approach remained largely redundant and self-referential, as well as often being counterproductive. The instrument of TACIS technical assistance projects demonstrated all its inconsistency on a practical level. The project management phases were often characterized by serious and repeated deviations, replicating the phenomena recorded elsewhere during the same period of entailing a systematic shift from "Project Cycle Management" to the multiple deviations of a worst practice model of "Project Circus Management" (Pellicciari 2022a: 51–53; Wedel, 2001). Proof of this was the scarcity of results and performance achieved by the projects launched to support the implementation of the new cooperation framework; examples of the aforesaid lack of success included multi-million Euro contracts such as "Support to TACIS Coordination Unit", "Support to PCA Implementation", and the "Ukrainian European Policy Legal Advice Centre".[6] Vague in their objectives and often set up with glaring design errors, these projects did not go beyond redundancy and unsustainable cosmetic interventions. Procured through EU tender procedures plagued by arbitrary practices, the implementation of these projects was entrusted to private consultancy companies that were often more interested in the profit coming from the management of the project budgets, than in the real achievement of non-mandatory project results. This was so as they were not held contractually accountable for the latter by the EU (Ibid.).

Despite the serious problems and red flags raised by the European Commission's internal monitoring reports, these projects were refinanced over the years in successive phases, with multi-million-euro contracts being awarded to the same small number of European consulting firms, notwithstanding their very poor track record in terms of sustainable results. Thus, the perception of European institutions as being weak and not really interested in achieving true reforms was cemented among Kyiv's leadership itself (Ibid.).

Unlike the EU, the US had a more strategic approach to the country during this period, and was more consistent in its programs. After an initially cautious start (in the period from 1991 to 1995, American assistance amounted to 1.05 billion ECU,[7] i.e., little more than one-third of European assistance), the US Congress officially declared the country a priority for American aid in the region; spending was set to begin as soon as the serious hyperinflation in Kyiv abated.

In the period from 2001 to 2004, USAID primarily financed such areas as the development of small and medium-sized enterprises, nuclear safety, governance, civil society, fiscal policy, healthcare, and others.[8] A mechanism for dialogue and cooperation at the highest level, the *Gore-Kuchma Commission*[9] was created, and Ukraine quickly became the third-largest recipient of US aid after Israel and Egypt.[10] However, business-oriented US programs were significantly better financed than those concerning other sectors such as the strengthening of democracy and the rule of law. Although the EU and the US quickly became Ukraine's largest partners and donors, this reduced activity on the political-institutional level, and the renunciation by the aforesaid to changing the *status quo* provided a large window of opportunity for Russian influence in Ukraine for well over a decade.

The Russian aid initiative in Ukraine, although vast in quantitative terms, was handled in a peculiar manner. Firstly, it subsidized Ukrainian business and the population via the reliable provision of cheap energy and raw material exports, as well as generous access to its markets. This Russian aid was not loaded with excessive political rhetoric and was taken for granted by the population in Ukraine, both because of the putative proximity between the Ukrainian and Russian leadership and the political-cultural climate of a persistent post-Soviet osmosis between the two countries. Subsequently, this investment would misfire for Russia.

On the one hand, cheap energy and market access forged Ukrainian oligarchs who immediately reinvested their Russian-sponsored capital in the Western economy; accordingly, their decision-making was biased by this mechanism. On the other hand, an illusion of artificial prosperity characterized by positive family-level planning was created for the Ukrainian population; this boosted Ukrainian demographics and curbed emigration, with many Ukrainians reacting by trying to imitate the lifestyles of the old European middle classes. This, despite having an incomparably inferior market position. As a result, the wealth that originated in Russian aid ironically created a bias in the mass beneficiaries thereof towards a pro-European orientation. Thereafter, no sentimentality would be shown toward Moscow for this period of prosperity enjoyed in the 2000s and first half of the 2010s.

Secondly, Russia inflated the personal wealth of a chosen few individuals in Ukraine so that they would foster a social base and a "neighborhood policy" accommodating Russian interests. The latter category consistently ignored governance, civil society, and institution-building activities, accumulating instead family and private capital. All the while, apt Ukrainian social achievers in the public sector who were neutral or even sympathetic to Russia were repeatedly cut off from Russian aid and became disillusioned with the Russian connection. Thus, Russia both missed strategic opportunities and squandered hundreds of billions of Euros in funds,[11] handing "the aid floor" for Ukraine back to the EU and the US.

Despite having been heavily downgraded in international grandeur during the dark 1990s, Russia considered the position of its naval fleet in Sevastopol, the transit and supply of its gas to Ukraine and Europe, and the elimination of Ukrainian nuclear weapons to be matters of overriding national interest. These priorities were reflected in the design of the Commonwealth of Independent States (CIS) which was established in 1991 and which – according to the CIS Charter[12] – was tasked with ensuring economic and social progress, by focusing on political and economic cooperation and security. Thus, until 2004, for a full 13 years after its independence, Ukraine remained in the Kremlin's orbit, at Russia's expense, in a steady state position that was *de facto* accepted by the EU and proved to be a key factor in the future Ukraine–Russian conflict.

2005–2010 The Pro-European Ambition

The second period coincided with the presidency of Viktor Jushenko, who was elected after the initial victory of the pro-Russian leader Viktor Yanukovich. The presidency of the latter politician was annulled following accusations of irregularities by the so-called Orange Revolution. The latter was a street movement strongly inspired by Euro-Atlantic convictions and political intolerance for Moscow. The primary affirmation of the Ukrainian national spirit in the Western area of the country over the pro-Russian regionalism in the East – resulted in a strong turn towards pro-Western orientation in foreign policy. This was manifested in Ukraine's very outspoken demand to strengthen cooperation with the European Union (Minakov et al., 2021; Kubicek, 2008; De Ploeg 2017).

For Kyiv, the goal of signing the coveted Association Agreement (AA) with Brussels was understood as an intermediate step towards soon finalizing full EU membership, a priority that had since 2004 been reiterated at the highest level during all Euro-Ukrainian and Eastern Partnership summits. Among the exogenous factors that reinforced this ambition was the historic breakthrough of the EU enlargement process in 2004, with the entry of ten new member states, among which were four former Warsaw Pact countries (Poland, Hungary, Czechia, and Slovakia), as well as three former Soviet republics (Lithuania, Latvia, and Estonia). However, while in the medium term these countries pushed for, and in part obtained, greater European attention towards the East, what prevailed in the immediate term was an attitude of great caution on the part of the EU. This behavior was inspired by some key member states (first and foremost Germany) which had been hesitant to set a precise schedule on the European agenda to favor EU enlargement encompassing Ukraine.

The recurring dynamic of this period was in the behavior of Brussels which, although it had opened bilateral negotiations with Ukraine for new association and free trade agreements, was, at the same time, delaying their finalization. Indeed, the EU continued to treat Kyiv in a manner that put it in line with the remaining ex-Soviet countries of the Eastern Partnership. On February 21, 2005 the EU–Ukraine Cooperation Council diverted the operational aid cooperation to the *EU–Ukraine Action Plan under the European Neighborhood Policy (ENP)*.[13] The Action Plan set out a more compensatory and ambitious framework for joint work. However, the fact that, as with the PCA in 1994, the ENP made Ukraine fall back into a European "neighboring" space (and therefore outside the EU) was a clear political signal that the prospect of a soon-to-be-finalized association agreement was being discouraged and that, in general, EU accession was an unattainable chimera for Kyiv.

The framework of European aid programs accurately reflected this political situation, and while there was a sharp increase in the funding allocated, the themes and instruments of intervention remained identical as those in the past; both on the part of the donor and the recipient decided reluctance existed to focus on structural reforms in line with the objectives formally sanctioned in the new agreements. From January 1, 2002 to September 30, 2009, the EC committed €832.8 million[14] for cooperation with Ukraine; meanwhile, in the period between 2005 and 2008, the EU and some individual Member States (Germany, Sweden, France, the UK and Austria) had contributed up to 40 percent of total donor commitments.[15] The lion's share of aid programs had still been geared towards economic and trade cooperation, while only 14.5 percent[16] of total support was allocated at that time to enact legal, administrative, and institutional reforms.

On the other hand, EU support for the Rule of Law, in particular the judiciary, which had been weak in the previous period, focused on improving the legislative framework for economic development and trade, assistance to the judiciary, and support for the reform of arbitration courts. In the eyes of the West the aforesaid package demonstrated the importance of an efficient national judiciary system capable of supporting economic development in the first place.

Despite more comprehensive support than in the previous period, these actions were still being implemented as TACIS technical assistance projects, replicating previously seen situations of redundancy and ineffectiveness, featuring a lack of transparency in the use of resources; the aforesaid as per several monitoring reports and independent evaluations conducted by the European Commission during this period (Ibid.).

After the EU, the United States was the second largest donor in terms of resources allocated, with financial commitments towards Ukraine representing 15.8 percent[17] of total aid in the same period. USAID's interventions also became sensitive to the themes of strengthening the Rule of Law and anti-corruption, which had been dealt with in a separate program that was funded with US$36 million in the period between 2006 and 2010.[18]

Washington's political support was particularly vigorous during the first phase of Yushchenko's presidency, the inauguration ceremony of whom was attended by both the US Secretary of State Colin Powell and the Secretary General of NATO Jaap de Hoop Scheffer. At that time, the pro-Western front in Kyiv still held a more markedly pro-Atlantic position like those developing in Georgia, i.e., subsequent to the Rose Revolution in November 2003. The second phase of his presidency saw the political weakening of Yushchenko subsequent to his eroding relationships within the government majority supporting him. This facilitated the return to the game of the pro-Russian component represented by Yanukovych's *Party of Regions*, strongly supported by a constant flow of direct financial aid from Moscow.

On an interesting note, pro-European orientation by Kyiv paradoxically represented for Moscow the most acceptable of the concrete pro-Western political options during the Yushchenko presidency. So much so that (also due to a coincidental constructive phase of political relations between Moscow and Brussels) cooperation with the European Union turned out to be a compromise solution that allowed pro-Western and pro-Russian positions to coexist (Ibid.).

At the same time, Russia increased its prices for natural resources; and though they remained well below market levels this was a move that, given the underdevelopment of the Ukrainian economy and combined with the 2008–2009 economic crisis and inflation, caused major economic issues. With Ukraine heavily dependent on its subsidized supplies of raw materials, Moscow remained determined to use them as an incentive to keep Kyiv within its sphere of influence. In the context described the lesser evil for Moscow was EU cooperation with Ukraine, given that it dealt with the economy, limited itself to window-dressing on political issues, and excluded *a priori* any kind of cooperation in the military area. It is therefore not surprising that this pro-European agenda was formally maintained with the return of the pro-Russian Yanukovych to government, first as Prime Minister from 2007 to 2008 and then as president after his victory in the 2010 elections. Moreover, the latter was facilitated by internal divisions within the pro-Western front, which arose precisely because of the divergence of views on the type of relations to be adopted with Russia (Kudelia, 2014; Mearsheimer, 2014).

It is noteworthy that in 2007 Ukraine joined[19] the Paris *Declaration on Aid Effectiveness*, which outlined several coordination, monitoring, and evaluation measures aimed at increasing the efficiency and effectiveness of Foreign Aid. However, no immediate mechanisms for donor coordination were established at the national level. Consequently, although a stronger political will to implement reform existed, real progress without an effective system of conditionalities and without clearly demonstrated ownership of Ukraine over the implementation of policies had yet to be achieved. Distracted by political rivalries and economic issues, the government in Kyiv was in practice unable to secure the necessary changes.

2010–2014 Aid War

For most of his term in office, Yanukovych tried to implement a dual-track policy that would allow him to reconcile the protection afforded by the primacy of Russian political influence with the considerable structural advantages of economic cooperation with the European Union; the aim was to lift the country out of the quite serious socio-economic crisis it was in (Ibid). It was a policy that Yanukovych conducted at his own initiative and at times it earned him rebuking calls from Moscow. This policy was conducted in the hopes of obtaining economic concessions from Brussels, e.g., a free-trade zone and a free visa regime. Otherwise, it simply replicated the *modus operandi* of the "aid without reforms" of the Kuchma period. During his electoral campaign, Yanukovych emphasized his intent to conduct tax and pension reforms; in the end such promises were only partially maintained (D'Anieri, 2003; Kudelia, 2014).

Combating corruption was, yet again, not high on the agenda.[20] At the same time, some concrete justice sector reforms were implemented regarding the rationalization of punishment for mischievous mass market economy practices, the westernization of criminal procedure, and the institution of self-regulation and responsibility in professional associations. Furthermore the normalization of remuneration for lay judges as a means of attracting quality candidates and enabling them to function without corruption, and the conduction of preparatory work for prosecutorial service reform were promoted. Still, reformist endeavors under the Yanukovych administration were kept on a separate plane from the policy recommendations of the EU and other Western donors, both bilateral and multilateral.

Having developed geo-political interest in Ukraine that, compared to the past, had grown hand in hand with direct involvement in the country's political and institutional affairs, Western donors were basically unwilling to support a pro-Russian government. Despite the fact that they were unable to reduce Russia's presence and operations in the country. Proof that the dimension of development and economic cooperation was no longer separate from domestic political issues became evident when business-oriented international institutions and organizations also became substantially more critical towards Kyiv.

As bribery remained common and raids on private property increased, from 2010 to 2014 Ukraine remained at the peak of the *Corruption Perception Index* (146th–144th);[21] meanwhile the *Index of Economic Freedom* indicated that:

> (...) at the peak of the economic crisis in November 2009 Ukraine was freer than in November 2011. The country was ranked last out of 43 countries in the European region, and its overall score is lower than the world average (...) Poor protection of property rights and widespread corruption discourage entrepreneurial activity, severely undermining prospects for long-term economic expansion. The rule of law is weak, and the judicial system remains susceptible to substantial political interference. Corruption and government intervention in the economy continue to undermine economic growth.[22]

The Government of Ukraine itself indicated that the key problems causing the ineffectiveness of the justice system were a "lack of judicial independence, pervasive corruption, and a complex and unwieldy judicial structure and court process". Furthermore, the fact that corruption was "pervasive and entrenched" was denounced.[23] Although Ukraine adopted the *National Anticorruption Strategy* for 2011–2015 and the *State Programme for Prevention and Combating Corruption* for the same period, the real implementation of these guidelines remained a challenge.

From the European Bank for Reconstruction and Development (EBRD) to the World Bank (WB), via the International Monetary Fund (IMF), which suspended the program launched in 2010 "because the results of the program have fallen short of expectations",[24] donors began to make aid conditional on the fulfilment of requirements that were not strictly economic. USAID strongly reduced the budget allocations for the period 2011–2013 (only €6.9 million),[25] still insisting on the application of Rule of Law and justice reform initiatives but choosing to support the local non-governmental sector. The latter mainly opposed the Yanukovich government. In the hopes of the return of pro-Western forces, these non-governmental sector support programs facilitated the growth of a new future political elite, among whom were several of the future protagonists of the Maidan revolution.

As concerns institutional cooperation, Western aid was *de facto* frozen, as it was tied to the fulfilment of stringent conditions by the recipient, some of which referred to specific episodes of political life in Kyiv. This was the case of the EU-Ukraine AA that was strongly desired by Yanukovich, the signing of which was suspended by Brussels in November 2012. Formally, this suspension was attributed to the politically motivated trial that Kyiv was carrying out against former pro-Western Prime Minister Yulia Tymoshenko.

To unblock the agreement and related aid, Brussels demanded wider guarantees of "electoral, judicial, and constitutional reforms" as well as the *de facto* release of Tymoshenko. After a year of concessions and hardening of positions, the dual-track policy became untenable for Kyiv. Under heavy pressure from Moscow, Yanukovich blatantly broke off negotiations with the EU and renounced European aid, to embrace Russian aid. On December 17, 2013, Ukraine signed a treaty with Russia in which the latter pledged to purchase $15 billion in Ukrainian bonds, and to supply its natural gas to Kyiv at a further reduced price.[26]

This treaty marked the final break in the difficult coexistence between pro-Russian political orientations and attempts to undertake economic cooperation with the West, triggering the Maidan protests that would lead to Yanukovich's forced ousting, followed by his flight to Russia. The aforesaid episode marked the emergence of a long-standing geo-political competition between the West and Russia on the terrain of their assistance policies towards countries and in areas of common strategic interest. From this perspective, Ukraine in 2014 was the most visible scenario of what had been the global *Aid War* aimed at redefining international balances and related spheres of influence in the post-Cold War period (Trebesch et al., 2023; Bosse, 2022; Dräger, Gründler, and Potrafke, 2022; Pishchikova, 2010; Woehrel, 2014).

2014–2022 The Atlanticist Strategy

The last period refers to the eight years preceding the outbreak of war and includes the entire presidency of Petro Poroshenko and part of the term of Volodymyr Zelensky, who succeeded him in

May 2019. It was a period marked by the radicalization of the internal clash between the pro-Western and pro-Russian options, aggravated by waning opportunities for domestic political dialogue between the two options.

After the Maidan revolution, the new Ukrainian government witnessed an unchallenged return to the original positions of the Orange Revolution, namely pro-Western bias and clear, frontal opposition to the Kremlin. Thus, the political maneuvering space of the pro-Russian option, orphaned after Yanukovich's flight, was effectively limited. Among other things, extensive constitutional amendments introduced in 2016 cemented Ukraine's resolve to develop along European and Euro-Atlantic lines.

On the other hand, with the annexation of Crimea to the Russian Federation and the intensification of guerrilla warfare in the Donbas area, the pro-Russian option withdrew from Kyiv and ceased to have a national political profile, shrinking even within the Russian-speaking regions controlled by Ukraine.

The donors followed this internal polarizing trend and indeed stimulated and contributed to accentuating it, bringing the historic competition between Western and Russian aid to a new level of geo-political clash, which degenerated into episodic military confrontation in the areas of the Donbas. Western donors' interventions were combined in the spirit of convinced support and reinforcement of the pro-Western/anti-Russian position taken by Kyiv, with a substantial increase in aid allocations. All with greater conviction than that shown at the time of the Orange Revolution.

Integrated programs were launched with the more ambitious direct objectives of an overtly political-institutional nature in areas previously touched upon marginally or with little conviction.

Unlike during the previous periods under examination, the increased aid was supplemented with clear conditionalities and regulatory frameworks.

For example, the EC opinion[27] on Ukraine's EU candidacy provided seven very specific conditions to be fulfilled by Ukraine by the end of 2022, all of which were related to Rule of Law and Justice reform. These areas became primary sectors and key words in all new Western interventions.

The EU-Ukraine AA,[28] signed after the Maidan revolution, set the framework for the expected Ukrainian reforms, particularly in Title III of the agreement "Justice, Freedom and Security".

In addition, annual reports on the implementation of the EU–Ukraine AA were introduced to assess the progress of reforms; these evaluations highlighted achievements as well as persisting challenges and pitfalls.

Rule of Law, the adoption of institutional reforms, and the reduction of endemic corruption in Ukraine also became key priorities for the EBRD,[29] the IMF,[30] and the WB in their attempts to strengthen non-state institutions and advocate for the fair treatment of businesses. The establishment of an independent Business Ombudsperson was part of the latter initiative.

The main point is that reforms which stalled during the tumultuous period from November 2013 to February 2014 resumed their course with gusto, though not always with the efficiency promised. A major reform of the prosecution system was accomplished, building on the preparatory work of the previous administration. Post-Soviet *obshchy nadzor* (general oversight) competence was finally eliminated, which had both been a major source of corruption and a protective shield for the country's oversized public sector. Judicial reform progressed considerably; it featured better and institutionalized judicial self-government and the re-establishment of a consolidated Supreme Court, vesting the latter with power to establish generally binding legal positions as an island of common law atop the judicial system. Furthermore, this reform aimed to recruit anew the members of its judiciary, in a highly publicised attempt at open competition during the recruitment process. A further reform vetted all the country's judges through professional exams and interviews.

However, following an increasingly characteristic "two-steps forward-two-steps back" tradition, eligible professionals without elite backgrounds or powerful connections faced a glass ceiling during the selection of the Supreme Court justices', though the newly recruited judges proved to be younger and decisively more modern. Among them, the more professional and ethical judges had bigger issues passing the vetting process. An ambitious civil service reform showed mixed success, establishing "islands" of effective Western-educated bureaucrats at the top level of most ministries and agencies and creating vacant postings in the executive branch public. All the while professionals working their way up from the bottom were disadvantaged, which enabled an unhealthy dichotomy of unaccountable privileged beneficiaries *versus* lower-ranked civil servants overburdened by most of the work and deprived of career and training opportunities. In National Unification reforms, with the strengthening of pro-Ukrainian language policies and the attempt to establish a national church, complex cultural issues were addressed through a simple top-bottom regulatory approach. The five undisputed pivotal reforms were: (a) the partial re-building of the army; (b) the streamlining of public services dealing with legal documents and records; (c) the modernization of local self-government under the principles of state rescaling and subsidiarity; (d) an education reform that emphasized individual education plans and the modernization of schooling in a "fit-for-real-life" direction; (e) and the long-overdue introduction of transparency in the public sector, as well as proper declaration of public officials' income (the latter reform would have meant so much if it had been introduced 25 years earlier, i.e., in 1991). Last but not least, serious resistance was shown towards the concrete application of several dedicated anti-corruption measures that had been introduced.

In all the spheres of reform and foreign aid that enabled them, the same main problem was visible: a rather weak commitment on behalf of the establishment in Kyiv and of the main regional centres. Occasional breakthroughs did occur due to the personal ambition and residual revolutionary zeal of the lone reformers who led the charge; though individual commitment was present in these instances, alas, equally exhibited at times were Machiavellian political manoeuvring and an *ad hoc* opportunism calculated to gain Western support.

The political wave of 2019 that led to the Zelenskyy phenomenon and his party's political monopoly over the legislative, executive, and judicial branches was initially characterized by frenzied activity to convert into law many legislative proposals that had been lying in government departments and advocacy NGOs for decades. These were passed with little or no parliamentary debate and without a technical-legal opinion from legislative offices.

For the record, the digitization of public services culminating in the pioneering "Diia" platform, and the codification of administrative procedure were clear successes. Likewise, the commodification of agricultural land, the adoption of an electoral code, and the finalization of regulation on secondary education may also arguably be considered positive changes. While some relevant legislation (such as in the environment and energy sector) was adopted in line with the *EU acquis*, many rent-seeking and plainly low-quality rules entered Ukraine's system, thus generating an already self-contradictory, increasingly chaotic, and inefficient legal system.

The only effect of the incomplete tax reform was mobilized political opposition, as it failed to make richer Ukrainians reconsider their mass, institutionalized tax evasion. Antitrust regulations such as the anti-oligarch law[31] were greatly featured in public relations campaigns but proved unnoticeable in the application phase. This time, just as under the previous administration, reactionary forces were quick to reinstate the existing equilibrium even before the 2022 war, with the political marshalling of constitutional justice, and the administration of extrajudicial "internal sanctions" against the country's own subjects. This was the reality that substituted for the due process of law in competent independent courts; indeed, since the beginning of the war, repression against freedom of speech in the media has increased and must be considered a sign of regression. However, despite such varied and serious changes, international aid to Ukraine does not seem to have been modified accordingly. The only visible changes have been the restructuring of EU aid, the discontinuation of programs at the micro and meso-level, and the concentration of financial assistance on a macro-level around 2020. Otherwise, international aid has continued to flow towards Ukraine regardless of the lack of much-needed reform.

Loaded with high symbolic value and perceived as an expression of Western assertiveness over Russia, these aid initiatives were acknowledged merely because they existed and were de-emphasized compared to the aims announced. This led to an *impasse* in which, on the one hand, the recipient, aware of its strategic importance for the donors, was reassured by its Euro-Atlantic orientation and thus resisted reforms to deal with the country's systemic problems, from corruption in the public sphere to the osmosis between political and economic oligopolies. On the other hand, the donors, while not sparing these poor results from criticism, tolerated the situation and avoided raising the level of controversy out of fear of geopolitical jeopardization of the West's political relationship with Kyiv.

The 2017 Organization for Economic Cooperation and Development (OECD) Fourth Assessment Report stated[32] that:

> (...) the most urgent challenge for Ukraine is to ensure the sustainability of the institutional framework and to strengthen anti-corruption efforts, which are constantly undermined by the ruling elite. Recent measures to discourage anti-corruption activism are alarming and must be stopped as a matter of urgency.

The fact that the EU–Ukraine AA came into force in 2017, only three years after it was signed in 2014, is indicative of the persistence of the usual Brussels–Kyiv dynamic. The latter was held back by some of its member states from taking real steps toward Ukraine's EU membership, while on the contrary Kyiv loaded every step of its relationship with Brussels with clear expectations of EU membership (Minakov et al., 2021; Kubicek, 2008; Subtelny, 2009).

Despite frequent criticism of the real progress made on reform in the annual reports issued on the implementation of the EU–Ukrainian AA, the country has been flooded with an unprecedented amount of aid. The AA was followed by five consecutive Macro-Financial Assistance (MFA) operations totalling €5 billion in loans over the period between 2015 and 2021 and was claimed to be the largest amount of MFA the EU has ever disbursed to a single partner country.[33] In addition to the ENI, Ukraine benefited from several cooperation projects in a wide range of sectors and assistance under specific EU instruments, ranging from the Instrument Contributing to Stability and Peace (IcSP) to the Instrument for Democracy and Human Rights (EIDHR).

According to the Implementation Report of the EU–Ukraine AA for 2021, the EU (together with the European financial institutions) have mobilised over €17 billion in grants and loans since 2014 (exceeding the commitment of €11.175 billion made in 2014). In general, the Implementation Report stated that:

> the Rule of Law and fight against corruption remained, justifiably, at the centre of reform efforts and engagement with international partners, including as regards critical reform of Ukraine's judiciary. Implementation of key reforms adopted [in 2021], such as the reform of the High Council of Justice

and High Qualifications Commission of Judges, thus remains a litmus test for broader reform efforts and for Ukraine's further progress in its democratic and strategic European orientation.[34]

It was the European allocations in the areas of institution building, strategic planning and the coordination of public policies, the fight against corruption, and the autonomy of the judiciary that gave a sense of both the focus on the timing of Ukraine's democratic transition, as well as the lack of impact on the ground.

This aid was delivered in the classic form of technical assistance projects (the "Anti-Corruption Initiative" had a budget of over €37 million, while the "Pravo–Justice" project alone totaled €25 million). The aforesaid projects, set in the Ukrainian political-institutional context, suffered from internal conflicts, high local turnover at the top of the ranks of the civil service administration and general political aversion to embracing structural changes. Despite poor results and redundant activities in the face of large allocations, even these projects were maintained and refinanced, protected by the climate of political partnership created between donor and recipient.

Within this general political framework of Western assistance, however, an important divergence is present between the dynamics of Europeanism and Atlanticism, respectively promoted by the European Union and the United Kingdom, the United States, and their Central European allies. Additionally, NATO can be counted among the latter category, though to a lesser extent. If Ukraine's pro-European perspective and founded hopes for NATO membership continued to exist, both of the country's strategic constitutional objectives continued to clash with the scepticism of an indulgent West over a fast-paced integration of Ukraine. However, the path taken in the Atlanticist direction was a different matter, particularly after the annexation of Crimea to the Russian Federation and the proxy war in the Donbas.

At the initiative of London, Washington, Warsaw and the Baltic capitals, concrete steps were intensified towards an ever-closer consolidated axis with Ukraine, the first operational result of which generated *concrete military* cooperation programs and aid to Kyiv. Their primary goal was to increase the capabilities of the Ukrainian army and set up strategic coordination between

Kyiv and the "Intermarium quartet", the UK and the US through NATO, to contain Russian influence in Eastern Europe.

The consistency and linearity of the *Intermarium + Atlanticist* path, compared to the Europeanist one, led Kyiv to burden the former with greater strategic importance. In the face of the deteriorating crisis in the Donbas, and despite its ritual proclamations that EU membership remained its number one priority, Kyiv engaged in strong substantive foreign policy coordination with NATO, especially with the activist NATO member states. This state of affairs continued uninterrupted until the outbreak of the war in 2022 (Strazzari, 2022; Wolff, 2015: 1103–1121; Sperling and Webber, 2017).

As for Russia's aid, it has followed two seemingly contradictory strategies, which have actually fed off one another. Following the logic of frontal confrontation, since 2014 and well before the military invasion, Moscow has provided a substantial framework of financial, military, logistical, and humanitarian aid to the eastern regions, in open confrontation with Kyiv.

In this way, Russia bore the costs of what was already interpreted as a *de facto* secession from Ukraine, even if this was not recognized by international law.

The interesting and often underestimated aspect of this situation, however, is that even during this phase of extreme polarization and guerrilla warfare, of occasional direct military clashes between the regular army formations of the two countries (such as those that occurred in 2014–2015 occurred in Ilovaisk and Debaltseve), Moscow continued to maintain an important diplomatic office in Kyiv.

Perhaps even more surprising is that it has continued to act as a *de facto* donor, without ceasing to supply Ukraine with energy exports. While increasing in price, the latter in the years leading up to the war remained well below the selling price on the international market.

Notes

1 Communication from the EU Commission to the EU Council "Action Plan for Ukraine" COM(96)523final of 20.11.1996 https://eur-lex.europa.eu/legal-content/EN/TXT/PDF/?uri=CELEX:51996DC0593&rid=9

2 EU-Ukraine Strengthening the Strategic Partnership. MEMO/05/57 of 23.02.2005. https://ec.europa.eu/commission/presscorner/detail/en/MEMO_05_57
3 Partnership and Cooperation Agreement Between EU and Ukraine. MEMO/94/38. https://ec.europa.eu/commission/presscorner/detail/en/MEMO_94_38
4 Ibid.
5 EU Action Plan on Justice and Home Affairs in Ukraine. Official Journal of the European Union, 29.03.2003. https://eur-lex.europa.eu/legal-content/EN/TXT/PDF/?uri=CELEX:52003XG0329(01)&from=EN
6 Monitoring Review of the Tacis NP Monitoring Program Ukraine, October 2005. https://europa.eu/capacity4dev/file/10296/download?token=JjoJ6p5k
7 Communication from the EU Commission to the EU Council "Action Plan for Ukraine" COM(96)523final of 20.11.1996. https://eur-lex.europa.eu/legal-content/EN/TXT/PDF/?uri=CELEX:51996DC0593&rid=9
8 ForeignAssistance.gov. www.foreignassistance.gov/cd/ukraine/2010/obligations/1
9 R. Lyle. "Ukraine: Pushing For Success With Kuchma-Gore Commission". 09.05.1997. www.rferl.org/a/1084759.html
10 Communication from the EU Commission to the EU Council "Action Plan for Ukraine" COM(96)523final of 20.11.1996. https://eur-lex.europa.eu/legal-content/EN/TXT/PDF/?uri=CELEX:51996DC0593&rid=9
11 Деловой Петербург. "Россия вложила в Украину в 50 раз больше денег, чем США". 22.04.2014 www.dp.ru/a/2014/04/22/Rossija_vlozhila_v_Ukrainu.
12 Charter of the Commonwealth of Independent States (with declaration and decisions). Adopted at Minsk on 22.01.1993.–https://treaties.un.org/doc/Publication/UNTS/Volume%201819/volume-1819-I-31139-English.pdf
13 EU-Ukraine Strengthening the Strategic Partnership. MEMO/05/57 of 23.02.2005. https://ec.europa.eu/commission/presscorner/detail/en/MEMO_05_57
14 Evaluation of the European Commission's Cooperation with Ukraine, Final Report. Volume 1: Main Report, December 2010. www.oecd.org/derec/ec/47272956.pdf
15 Ibid.
16 Ibid.
17 Ibid.
18 ForeignAssistance.gov. www.foreignassistance.gov/cd/ukraine/2010/obligations/1

19 Указ Президента України "Про приєднання України до Паризької декларації щодо підвищення ефективності зовнішньої допомоги" від 19.04.2007 N 325/2007. https://zakon.rada.gov.ua/laws/show/325/2007#Text
20 N. Kholod. Reforming the Ukrainian Economy under Yanukovych: The First Two Years, Carnegieendowment.org, 02.04.2012 https://carnegieendowment.org/2012/04/02/reforming-ukrainian-economy-under-yanukovych-first-two-years-pub-47702
21 Dashboards of the Corruption Perceptions Index. Trial International. www.transparency.org/en/cpi/2010
22 N. Kholod. Reforming the Ukrainian Economy under Yanukovych: The First Two Years. Carnegieendowment.org, 02.04.2012. https://carnegieendowment.org/2012/04/02/reforming-ukrainian-economy-under-yanukovych-first-two-years-pub-47702
23 Government of Ukraine Report on Diagnostic Study of Governance Issues Pertaining to Corruption, the Business Climate and the Effectiveness of the Judiciary. 11.07.2014. www.imf.org/external/pubs/ft/scr/2014/cr14263-a.pdf
24 IMF Country Report No.12/315. Ukraine, November 2012. www.imf.org/external/pubs/ft/scr/2012/cr12315.pdf
25 ForeignAssistance.gov. www.foreignassistance.gov/cd/ukraine/2010/obligations/1
26 K. Gorchinskaya. Russia gives Ukraine cheap gas, $15 billion in loans. Kyivpost.com, 17.12.2013. www.kyivpost.com/post/10469.
27 European Commission. Opinion on the EU membership application by Ukraine, 17.06.2022. www.google.com/url?sa=t&rct=j&q=&esrc=s&source=web&cd=&ved=2ahUKEwiPmsWt_NH8AhViXqQEHT82At0QFnoECA4QAQ&url=https%3A%2F%2Fec.europa.eu%2Fcommission%2Fpresscorner%2Fapi%2Ffiles%2Fdocument%2Fprint%2Fen%2Fqanda_22_3802%2FQANDA_22_3802_EN.pdf&usg=AOvVaw0UJdDvuf7UFEuyG5QwKTp_
28 Association Agreement between the European Union and its Member States, of the one part, and Ukraine, of the other part. Official Journal of the European Union, L161/3 of 29.05.2014. https://trade.ec.europa.eu/doclib/docs/2016/november/tradoc_155103.pdf
29 Ukraine Overview. European Bank of Reconstruction and Development. www.ebrd.com/where-we-are/ukraine/overview.html
30 Reforming the Judiciary: Learning from the Experience of Central, Eastern, and Southeastern Europe. www.google.com/url?q=https://www.imf.org/~/media/Files/Publications/REO/EUR/2017/November/eur-reo-chapter-2.ashx&sa=D&source=docs&ust=1674081915590202&usg=AOvVaw1jKiKyf57qp9F4oCFelwhq

31 The Law of Ukraine No. 1780-IX of November 5, 2021 on Preventing threats to national security associated with excessive influence by persons who wield significant economic and political weight in public life (oligarchs). www.venice.coe.int/webforms/documents/?pdf=CDL-REF(2021)086-e
32 OECD. Anti-corruption reforms in Ukraine. Fourth round of monitoring of the Istanbul Anti-Corruption Action Plan, 2017. www.oecd.org/corruption/acn/OECD-ACN-4th-Round-Report-Ukraine-ENG.pdf
33 European Commission. Commission Staff Working Document "Ex-ante evaluation statement accompanying the document Proposal for a Decision of the European Parliament and of the Council on providing macro-financial assistance to Ukraine", SWD(2022) 25 final of 01.02.2022. https://eur-lex.europa.eu/LexUriServ/LexUriServ.do?uri=SWD:2022:0025:FIN:EN:PDF
34 European Commission. Joint Staff Working Document "Association Implementation Report on Ukraine", SWD(2022) 202 final of 22.07.2022. www.eeas.europa.eu/sites/default/files/documents/Association%20Implementation%20Report%20on%20Ukraine%20-%20Joint%20staff%20working%20document.pdf

4 From Neutralist to Interventionist Aid

Ukraine 2022 vs Bosnia and Herzegovina 1992

To capture the characteristics of the IAPPs in the Ukrainian conflict, the period observed herein is limited to the fourteen months following the outbreak of the war triggered by the Russian invasion on February 24, 2022. To benefit from a comparative method that captures its salient aspects, the Ukrainian war case must be placed side-by-side with another one as similar as possible in terms of macro-historical period, geographical location, and protagonists.

Specifically, to make a comparison with Ukraine in 2022, one must refer to a concrete historical case that ideally has the following characteristics:

(a) it concerns a sovereign state that receives aid;
(b) it is located in the European geo-political space;
(c) it has experienced a war on its own territory;
(d) the conflict in (c) took place during the post-bipolar period; and
(e) the context ideally involved the same donors active in Ukraine.

The combination of these characteristics objectively limits the choice to the Western Balkan countries that – in the 1990s – were the scene of the last wars to be fought on European soil before the recent conflict in Ukraine. In particular, the reference herein is to the first year of the war in Bosnia and Herzegovina (BiH), which broke out in 1992: exactly three decades before the Ukrainian crisis (Gilbert, 2016: 717–29; Pickering, 2014: 31–43). The comparison between the two historical cases is based on a three-level

DOI: 10.4324/9781003382157-4

Table 4.1 Aid in the War Outbreaks in Ukraine (2022) and in Bosnia and Herzegovina (1992)

	BiH 1992	Ukraine 2022
Scenario		
Domestic	• Provisional sovereignty • Weak and divided state • Country divided into three sub-states • Incidence of endogenous factors • Civil war with conventional weapons	• Consolidated sovereignty • Institutionalized statehood • Tension centred/ West–East • Incidence of exogenous factors • War between armies with hybrid and tactical weapons
International	• Uncertain international context • Fragmented diplomatic action • New and unknown scenario	• A Big Game scenario • Defined geo-political interests. • Key players long active and present in the country
Actors		
Donors	• Primacy of Specialized Multilateral agencies/ NGO sector	• Primacy of Western Bilateral Donors
Recipients	• New, occasional, fragmented	• Single recipient, Government/Pre-war Partner of the Donors
Aid		
Historical Precedents	• No pre-war IAPPs track record	• Recipient of IAPPs since 1991
Political Structure	• Neutralist: mitigate war effects • Limited/ Donor driven and managed humanitarian/ emergency • Third-world modalities of action	• Interventionist: achieve clear political objectives • Consistent/co-managed by recipient • Wide-ranging (financial, political, military) • Eight structural peculiarities

analysis of key elements in framing the history of IAPPS and politics, namely:

(a) *the scenario*: the domestic and international context in the run-up to and during the outbreak of war;
(b) *the actors*: donors and recipients, focusing on those present in both historical cases; and
(c) *the aid provided*: main political and technical characteristics of aid interventions.

Bosnia and Herzegovina 1992: A Perfect Storm

In order to frame the 1992 war scenario in BiH, we first must consider the context of the preceding years in which the origins of the conflict matured. They are located at the crossroads of domestic and international ruptures that first shook and then led to the break-up of the Socialist Federal Republic of Yugoslavia (SFRY) founded by Josip Broz Tito in 1946 (Radeljić, 2012; Craven, 1995: 333–413; Carmichael, 2015). Feeding off one other, these ruptures created the conditions for a perfect storm and the slide towards the point of no return of a serious political-institutional standoff.

The international context was marked by the sudden end to the bipolar order. The balance of power and the unstable equilibrium that for decades had governed the opposition between a Western and an Eastern front (respectively US- and Soviet-driven) broke down, thus determining the fall into irrelevance of the Non-Aligned Countries Movement, of which the SFRY had been one of the main drivers. During the decades of the Cold War the SFRY was recognized by both sides as constituting an indispensable buffer between the two constantly competing poles (Fagan, 2006: 406–19; Gilbert, 2016: 717–29; Hill, 2011).

In turn, in the European context, Yugoslavia ceased to be a useful geo-political clearing house between the Western and Eastern fronts. That position had for decades ensured that it was able to obtain substantial external aid from both poles to maintain its strategic sustainability and stability. This vertical loss of political importance and decline in international support had serious repercussions in Yugoslavia. Resources were lacking to maintain the very high costs of a redundant political-institutional organization which was inspired by a one-party communist ideology which, by definition, did not care about economic sustainability; this fact was worsened by its being a Federation. The latter characteristic in particular led Yugoslavia to a consociated multiplication of waste, and the dispersion of resources for each of the subjects federated to the SFRY (Carmichael, 2015). The disappearance of the ideological glue represented by the Communist Party and given that simultaneously the first multi-party internal electoral campaigns were conducted along ethnic lines only served to strengthen that bias within each federated entity. On the international front, the initial hypotheses of maintaining Yugoslavian statehood through a Confederation-type reorganization of the State gradually lost popularity, while the orientation of supporting the independentist demands of the individual federated subjects grew stronger.

Against the backdrop of the Yugoslav federal model, the BiH broke away from the SFRY, which was strongly opposed to by the Bosnian Serb Democratic Party (SDS). The latter, together with the other two formations with strong ethnic-religious connotations – respectively the Croatian Catholic (HDZ) and Bošnjak Muslims (SDA) – had formed the government that in 1990 emerged victorious from the first multiparty elections in the Socialist Republic of Bosnia and Herzegovina federated to SFRY. Nonetheless, following in the footsteps of Croatia and Slovenia, the Sarajevo government adopted a declaration of sovereignty (October 15, 1991), followed by a referendum that overwhelmingly declared independence (February 29/ March 1, 1992) despite the fact that 34 percent of rightful claimants, almost all of whom were Bosnian Serbs, had failed to vote (Rogel, 1998; 2004).

As this formal process of independence came to fruition, it crystallized internal divisions instead of resolving them, leading to the strengthening of self-declared sub-state entities that – *de facto* – detached themselves from Sarajevo, i.e., respectively, the Serbian Republic of Bosnia and Herzegovina and the Croatian Community of Herzeg-Bosnia (Glaurdić, 2011, Jović, 2009, Rogel, 1998; 2004). The Sarajevo government remained the only internationally recognized interlocutor; but the initial sovereignty of the country was very fragile with hardly any central institutions, particularly with regard to the Serbian and Croatian entities. Particularly in relations with the two Serbian and Croatian entities. Institutional chaos ensued in a country divided into three openly clashing parts, each with its own weak, but distinct, state organizations.

The start of the war, commonly dated to coincide with the beginning of the siege of Sarajevo and the declaration of independence of BiH (March 3, 1992) is actually a conventional date. Rather, the conflict was the result of a progressive slide which led to the escalation of increasingly bloody incidents and clashes, mainly by the Bosnian Serbs and the large parts of the former Yugoslav army they controlled (Ibid.). The scenario of the first year of the war further complicated the situation, exacerbating the existing divisions and burdening them with a dramatic humanitarian emergency. The conflict that resulted resorted to ethnic cleansing as a strategy of conquest and territorial consolidation; this claimed numerous victims, especially among civilians unable to flee. Each of the three ethnic-territorial components was engaged in organizing itself militarily and strengthening its own armies, making extensive recourse to para-military divisions that often acted with total operational autonomy and claimed local political-administrative powers over large parts of the country.

With the increasing involvement of Serbia and Croatia in the conflict, the scenario was aggravated by the fact that it constituted both an ethnically motivated civil war and a conflict between three former Yugoslav states (Croatia, BiH, and Serbia). From a tactical point of view, the initial phase of the conflict was tense, fast-moving, and violent, with the front lines being defined and subject to sudden reversals: militarily, the Bosnian Serbs led offensive efforts in the field, asserting their superiority based on Belgrade's military back up.

Internationally, the situation in BiH prior to the war was affected by the post-bipolar framework described above, as well as a decades-old system of equilibria that had to be redefined from scratch. The old-world order had broken down without another ready to replace it, and all the uncertainty about the future of the Western Balkans spilled over heavily onto BiH. The formal and geopolitical reorganization of what was to be the country with the most complex ethnic composition in the SFRY earned it the nickname "Little Yugoslavia" which became the subject of heated debate among the main players on the international scene (Ibid.).

Although 1992 opened with the belief that recognition of BiH's sovereignty within its former federal borders was imminent, among the main international actors there existed a widespread perception of the instability and temporariness of the *status quo*. Furthermore, there was a strong diversity of views about the changes to which BiH should be subjected, which were, in any case, seen as inevitable. In the international community, dominated by the countries of the Western bloc after the end of the Warsaw Pact, and the irrelevance of the Non-Allied Countries Movement, traditional national interests moved independently. These sought to carve out and consolidate priority zones of influence among the new Balkan areas that had again become geo-politically accessible in the post-bipolar era. The result was a dense network of bilateral initiatives at the political-diplomatic level that lacked a common direction and were oriented towards the former Yugoslav federal republics. Starting with BiH. They fueled uncoordinated centrifugal thrusts that limited the maneuvering space of multilateral institutions, underlining their limited political legitimacy and ineffectiveness in operating as concerned *crisis prevention*.

The months leading up to the war were characterized by the obvious political impotence of the United Nations as well as Brussels. At the time the latter was still the European Economic Community. Both subjects failed to contain the growing tension in BiH, i.e., to prevent it from degenerating into an out-of-control military confrontation (Ibid.). This international picture changed little in the initial period of the war, with the international community unable to express, and even less able to impose, its own common position. This inability rendered it culpably late in recognizing and attributing due importance to the scale of the spiraling violence taking place on the ground. The fact that the international community persisted on working on political solutions which were destined to inaction due to crossed vetoes led it to underestimate the explosive humanitarian dimension of the crisis. It follows that this caused it to remain silent, or nearly so, about dire episodes of civilian massacres, mass graves, torture, and rape; the news of such violations struggled to find space in the media in a manner proportionate to the gravity of the situation. The multilateral-institutional level did not go beyond formulating a few peace plans (Carrington-Cutileiro, Vance-Owen, and Owen-Stoltenberg) that had been overtaken by events on the ground before they were even formalized; meanwhile, on the bilateral level, single informal initiatives continued to be taken, particularly by Western European states (Ibid.).

In the perspective of a comparison with the international context of the war in Ukraine, it is useful to remark on the political-diplomatic role of the United States and Russia in BiH in 1992. With regard to the former, we were at the beginning of the United

States' monopolar decade commonly identified as the period in which Washington exercised the role of "world policeman". US foreign policy, which remained unchallenged on the scene in the post-bipolar dawning, dominated and directed international relations in a solitary manner. Nevertheless, unlike European diplomacies, Washington initially followed the evolution of the situation on the ground in the Western Balkans without considering direct involvement. That area was not a priority for US diplomatic action in Europe.

In complete continuity with the approach inherited from the Ronald Reagan Administration, which had been a protagonist in the 1980s of the most intense period of Russian-American relations, the main actors of the George Bush Administration focused on dealing with the consequences of the surprising and unexpected dissolution of the USSR. Above all, US diplomacy was intent on following the events of Russia's complex post-Soviet transition, which it carefully observed lest the collapse of the USSR – in itself a positive event – should create global instability that would be difficult to control. The remaining US diplomatic resources were being channeled towards the new sovereign states that had emerged since the dissolution of the USSR, as well as the geo-political areas of the former Warsaw Pact that had emerged under direct Soviet influence. The Western Balkans did not belong to either of these aforesaid categories (Ibid.).

Even more striking was the absence of a role for post-Soviet Russia in the Balkan context. If, in the US case, the initial relative lack of interest resulted from geopolitical priority choices, Moscow's inaction was because of its lack of resources and the collapse of Russia's international status brought about by the difficult post-Soviet transition. The profound social and economic crisis that the country experienced throughout the 1990s had strong political repercussions; this was true both at home, where a sense of anarchy and total weakness of organized power reigned, as well as at the international level, where the chronic lack of resources to support and renew the mammoth diplomatic and military network inherited from the USSR was responsible. Russia was perceived as being redundant, was left to its own devices and remained unguided. Faced with Yugoslav requests for back up from Belgrade during the break-up process, Moscow was unable to go beyond formulating messages of encouragement and vague solidarity that were not maintained by concrete political-military support for Serbia (Ibid.).

Neutralist Aid

The initial protagonists of aid were affected by this framework of uncertainty over the country's future geo-political position and bilateral diplomatic competition from the main international players of the time. Faced with the Western countries' reluctance to move and penchant for political tactics, the first donors to become active in the dramatic escalation of the Bosnian conflict came from the non-governmental sector of Western Europe. Alongside them, the others in the field were specialized agencies of classic international organizations traditionally active in emergency crises such as the *UN High Commissioner for Refugees* (UNHCR) or the *European Commission Humanitarian Organization* (ECHO). Their common trait lay in concentrating their efforts on emergency humanitarian aid, called upon to cover the quite serious lack of basic resources among most of the civilian population.

Attracted by the proximity of the crisis scenario and given the ease with which the region could be accessed by land, even by small organizations with limited budgets, the non-governmental sector moved with a galaxy of actors of various sizes. The more structured actors with a track record of professional interventions in other crisis scenarios often worked in coordination with and/ or were funded by the multilateral agencies themselves, on whose behalf they acted as implementing agencies. The novelty, however, was represented by a multitude of very small actors gaining their first experience in the field; these were newly established or had, during previous crises such as the first Gulf war, limited themselves in their respective countries to organizing fund-raising for the traditional international humanitarian organizations. Non-governmental interventions were often disconnected from one another, symbolic, and clearly unable to cope with the magnitude of the fractures and needs of the first year of war. Nevertheless, they had important political effects (Gilbert, 2016: 717–29; Pickering, 2014: 31–43; Hill, 2011).

Firstly, they made Western public opinion aware of the very serious humanitarian implications of a crisis otherwise neglected by the *mainstream* in the pre-social media era, and they indirectly put pressure on the leadership of their respective countries to become more actively involved in the scenario, at least in terms of aid. It is to this action that we owed the creation of a climate of solidarity favorable to the reception in Western Europe of large numbers of refugees and displaced persons from all over the former Yugoslavia. Acting unchallenged in the field, these donors had an easy time determining the predominant political narrative associated with aid, making them the almost exclusive bearers of *pacifist* messages, based on clear ideological stances rejecting the recourse to military solution. This position was absolute and even denounced military actions in self-defense. The recurring non-governmental call for "Aid for Peace" went hand-in-hand with a political neutralism that, in the name of caring for the victims of war regardless of ethnic, political, or territorial criteria, believed that it was not necessary to take sides in the ongoing crisis or with the warring parties (Pellicciari, 2022b; Hansen, 2006; Hill, 2011).

The aid provided by international agencies was obviously more structured in terms of hardware and better organization, though it nevertheless suffered equally high rates of dispersion and inefficiency of allocated resources. This was largely due to having to operate in a war scenario that was, by definition, complex and unstable and in which it was impossible to plan. That status quo was the daily reality, to the extent that the agencies were equipped with facilitated procurement rules and procedure. Thus, they had the spending capacity to cope with continuous emergencies and unforeseen day-to-day events – however this led to an enormous amount of money being spent without any control resulting in a devious misuse of funds. Furthermore, there was the almost insurmountable problems represented by the weakness of local aid recipients. While it was clear that the victims of war should be the recipients of humanitarian aid, the situation in the country made it extremely difficult to identify local counterparts with whom to negotiate.

The presence of three separate and conflicting state systems, political in nature but exercising weak governance and administrative impact on their respective territories, brought chaos at the central level and a wide heterogeneity of situations at the local level, i.e., in the individual municipalities. Complicating this picture was the very recent debut of Sarajevo's sovereignty hitherto unknown to the international community in its political and institutional components. This underlined the serious absence of even a minimal pre-existing network of diplomatic and institutional contacts with Bosnian institutions to whom donors could refer (Pellicciari, 2022a; Gilbert, 2016: 717–29; Pickering, 2014: 31–43).

However, systemic causes of aid dispersion also included political reasons internal to the donors. Firstly, there was, on the part of the multilateral agencies, the difficulty of acting for the first time in a country about which little or nothing was known; furthermore, operating in a scenario unfamiliar to them, in an environment that had entered a crisis for political reasons, and that featured high levels of socio-economic development was arduous. These circumstances highlighted all the limitations in mechanically transporting to BiH types of interventions honed during the previous decades in developing Third World scenarios. (Ibid.).

Moreover, the agencies suffered from the lack of a clear political mandate, with a consequent limitation of engagement rules due to their headquarters being blocked by internal competition and cross-vetoes; the diversity of views among their member states caused that blockage. As a result, their actions were placed on a strictly a-political plane, far removed even from the pacifism of the non-governmental sector, the active neutrality of which was replaced by an attitude of equidistance from the parties in the conflict, featuring deliberately ambiguous boundaries; this, to the extent that the majority of multilateral donors at the time interacted indistinctly with all parties and territories involved in the conflict. They operated not only with the three realities in BiH but also in Serbia, though Belgrade was already well on the brink of rupture with the Western world, having been accused of triggering the (para)military escalation of the Western Balkans crisis.

This "operational-functional" multilateralism calibrated only to the mandate of the aid to be implemented meant that, despite their direct experience in the field, the agencies as well as the local recipients of their actions were almost excluded from the international diplomatic policymaking process. Meanwhile the latter was vainly concerned with finding a solution to the crisis. In other words, not only did dealing with aid not guarantee one a voice, but it actually led donors active in the field to be excluded from the decision-making process on the main initiatives needed to end the conflict in the Western Balkans.

Ukraine 2022: A Big Game Scenario

Already at a first glance, the overall picture of Ukraine in 2022 appears rather different from that of BiH in 1992, starting with the marked osmosis and interpenetration between the domestic and international contexts that developed in the decades following the country's independence.

Compared to the Bosnian crisis, Ukraine presents differences that can be grouped into four systemic features, two each in the international and in the domestic context:

- *International relevance*
  - Geo-political importance for foreign key players;
  - Central issue on the international agenda;
  - Well-defined and determined geo-political interests;
  - High international media attention.

- *Incidence of exogenous factors*
  - External actors rooted and present on site;
  - Direct involvement of key players;
  - Influence on internal dynamics;
  - Kyiv is recognized by the West as a strategic partner.

- *Consolidated Ukrainian statehood*
  - Institutionalized state order;
  - Integrated subject in international relations;
  - Tensions concentrated in some regions.

- *Classical military warfare*
  - Start date of conflict;
  - Military clash between armies;
  - Use of tactical and hybrid weapons;
  - Most casualties in the army.

International Relevance

The real incidence and perceived geo-political importance of the Ukrainian scenario in the international system of reference is far greater than that of the Bosnian case in 1992. In the Western Balkans of the 1990s, zones of influence were being redefined from the remains of the former Yugoslavia, but it was only one of the scenarios, however dramatic, to open upon the collapse of communism in Eastern Europe, and not the main one geo-politically (Radeljić, 2012; Craven, 1995: 333–413). For the Western Balkans to become geo-politically central, one would have to wait for the conflict to end and the complex post-war and post-communist transition to begin. Ukraine, on the other hand, was already a big-game context from the outbreak of the war; this was affected by the growing climate of multipolar competition that pitted the Western front against the emerging Eurasian economic, demographic, and technological powers. Meanwhile the BRICS remained at the center (Minakov et al., 2021; Strazzari, 2022; Kubicek, 2005; De Ploeg, 2017; Subtelny, 2009). There was an immediate perception that US–China relations and the redefinition of balances from the Middle East to the Pacific depended on the development, duration, and final outcome of the conflict in Ukraine.

At the outbreak of the war, the internal tensions in Ukraine were already known to the international community and had long been at the center of its international agenda, while those in the Balkans had long been regarded as "internal issues of a sovereign state" about which very little was known and in which it was difficult to insert oneself from the outside; moreover, this was at a time when the conflict had already begun.

The Ukraine crisis was contextualized in the competition between the key players of the moment. Compared to the *Who-is-who*? *Who-wants-what*? and *Who-does-what*? confusion of the Balkans in the 1990s, the foreign actors confronting each other in Ukraine were well-defined, as were the objects of contention and the options and interests they brought to the table. Unlike Sarajevo, the political future of Kyiv was perceived to be a clear priority for the bilateral foreign policy of Washington and Moscow and the multilateral policy of the EU and NATO (Wolff, 2015: 1103–21; Sperling, Webber, 2017; Strazzari, 2022; Subtelny, 2009). Unlike the Western Balkans, Ukraine had – since 2014 – been *de facto* considered and treated as a country organically framed in the partnership system of the West. During the Bosnian war, Sarajevo was the country's capital in name only and became the victim of a siege that isolated it from the rest of the world. Kyiv, on the other hand, although subjected to periodic heavy Russian missile attacks, even in war remained the actual capital and a destination for many. Furthermore, it remained accessible for official visits by Western leaders and representatives accredited by the Ukrainian government.

The internationalization and geo-political importance of the scenario ensured that information provided to the Western public dedicated particular, constant coverage of Ukrainian events, starting from the Maidan revolution. When the war broke out, this media attention strengthened considerably, to maintain the involvement of public opinion with an intensity that (unfortunately) was not given to BiH, even during the most tragic episodes of the latter, such as the Srebrenica massacre or the Tuzla youth massacre.

War-related awareness was massive, including the presence of solidarity initiatives and campaigns in Western countries, including events ranging from the political to the economic, social, and cultural fields, as well as sporting events. However, reprising organizational formats already seen in other crises, these demonstrations of unity with Ukraine differed from the Bosnian case in that:

(1) These initiatives and popular campaigns were always able to count on effective and continuous support from public and institutional communication; in the Bosnian case, the intensity of the space devoted to the war in the media was much lower, despite the extremely high number of civilian victims. The latter were especially registered at the beginning of the conflict;
(2) In contrast to BiH, intense media exposure of the Ukrainian leadership, and in particular of President Zelensky, has not only increased the popularity of the country, but has also enhanced the international perception of its authority, raising it to considerably higher levels than in peacetime;
(3) Whereas in 1992 the Western bilateral actors had demonstrated reluctance to acknowledge the developing Bosnian conflict, thereby contributing to the aggravation of those dynamics, in 2022 those same actors unhesitatingly committed to promoting a public awareness campaign on the importance of urgently intervening in support of Kyiv (Radeljić, 2012; Craven, 1995: 333–413; Kubicek, 2005; De Ploeg, 2017; Subtelny, 2009).

As a result, within weeks of the start of the war, the entire Western public (even that portion which is generally more distracted) was aware of the main aspects of the Ukrainian issue, sensitized to the severity of the crisis, and updated daily and in real time about the development of events on the ground.

Unfortunately, the same attention had not been generated at the outbreak of the Bosnian war, where Western media coverage, that unchallenged and omnipresent source of information in the pre-digital age, had dedicated less intense coverage precisely of the initial phase of the war. Sadly, that was when the greatest number of civilian casualties occurred, caused by the ethnic cleansing suffered by the populations of the vast rural areas of BiH.

Incidence of Exogenous Factors

(1) The Ukrainian crisis was more susceptible to the influence of exogenous factors than the Bosnian crisis, which was determined by endogenous factors. This was true from the very origins of the conflict, triggered by an external factor *par excellence*, i.e. a military invasion by a foreign state. On the contrary, in BiH, the very nature of the ethnic clash underlined its predominantly internal genesis as a civil war, albeit one backed by new neighboring sovereign states. In comparison to BiH, all the international key players have long been active and present on the Ukrainian scenario. Indeed, the sides had already been in mutual competition there in the previous decades. They made use of their own structures on the ground, which were far more extensive than the classic diplomatic representations, with considerable expenditure of human and financial resources;

(2) This interest and presence in Ukraine allowed key players to exert influence on local socio-political dynamics, facilitating their open and direct involvement in internal affairs, in a manner unknown in BiH. Compared to the Western Balkans, these key external actors had a much higher and more established capacity to influence the dynamics of the Ukrainian political system, defining the major policy issues of the latter at the national level;

(3) The Western front has been engaged in strong and ongoing collaboration with Ukraine since 2014 and moreover shared

a common vision concerning the need to intervene immediately in support of the Kyiv government, featuring the latter as a privileged partner. In BiH, the lack of a clear local interlocutors with the donors, slowed down the determination of the latter to intervene in the war outbreak, to the extent that the Dayton Peace Accords took place almost four years after the symbolic beginning of the tragic siege of Sarajevo (Radeljić, 2012; Craven, 1995: 333–413; Kubicek, 2005; De Ploeg, 2017; Subtelny, 2009).

Consolidated Ukrainian Statehood

(1) In 2022, Ukraine boasted consolidated statehood; in contrast, the feeling of temporariness and weakness that hung over BiH in 1992 was striking. The Ukrainian state system benefitted from physiological institutionalization consolidated over thirty years of political-administrative life as an independent country prior to the war;
(2) Despite its internal democratization problems, Ukraine did not face the total institutional chaos of BiH, which was hit by a war simultaneous with its declaration of independence;
(3) At the international level, after the initial problems of resources and experience in the 1990s, a bilateral and multilateral diplomatic network developed, making Ukraine a sovereign state integrated into the international system and capable of expressing its own foreign policy. In 2022 Kyiv had for some years firmly held pro-Western and anti-Russian positions, supported in this by key multilateral players such as the EU and NATO. Instead, Sarajevo entered the war deprived of a clear international position and basically without an existing diplomatic network;
(4) The Central-Periphery tensions were regional in character, confined to a very specific area of Ukraine. By contrast, in BiH, tensions between the sides arose in a patchy fashion, throughout the entire national territory. Even when maximum confrontation was manifested, no one in Ukraine among the international policy analysts advancing various hypotheses on the future constitutional and\or territorial configuration of the country has questioned its survival as a sovereign state. Instead, even today, almost 30 years after the Dayton Peace

Accords, BiH is still under a formal international protectorate, and is the subject of discussion on what "final" form the country will have in the future, as if to underline the provisional nature of the current one (Ibid.).

Classic Military Warfare

(1) Compared to the Bosnian war featuring a strong ethnic component with patchwork-like distribution, the war in Ukraine broke out as a classic military conflict. Beginning with its clear start date of February 24, 2022, when Russian armored vehicles entered Ukrainian territory;
(2) War developments and military strategies in 2022 reflected a classic war between two states, rather than a predominantly ethnically based civil war in the Western Balkans. Initially, this could be seen in Moscow's attempt to replicate the rapid annexation of Crimea in 2014, with an intelligence operation aimed at co-opting centres of the Ukrainian armed forces and gaining their support for a sudden regime-change in Kyiv. Having dissipated the prospect of a "blitzkrieg" (apparently also thanks to Western counter-intelligence action which had been intensified in Kyiv after the Maidan revolution), for the remainder of 2022 the war saw two structured armies facing each other openly. Furthermore, their connections with their governmental leaderships in Kyiv and Moscow were direct and observed hierarchical discipline. There was no room for the autonomous territorial paramilitary units seen in BiH, to the extent that volunteers or contractors who joined one side or the other were recruited into respective armed forces. Even in the extremely rare cases of formally private armies such as the Wagner Group of Evgenij Prighozin, their members did not exercise exclusive control over clearly identified war-scarred territories, i.e., not answering to any military hierarchy. In contrast, in the Bosnian conflict these strong paramilitary dynamics had affected all parties involved in the conflict: from the Serbian *Tigers* of Željko Ražnatović, i.e. "Arkan", to the Croatian *Punishment Battalion* of Mladen Naletilić, i.e. "Tuta", to the military units of Muslim Bošnjak commander Naser Orić (Rogel, 1998);

Towards the end of 2022, the war was being fought with military strategies involving an extensive use of tactical and hybrid weaponry, in a war scenario of attrition where little was left to chance; the scene described was destined to become a textbook case for strategic-military studies, on a par with other previous highly tactical wars such as the 1973 fourth Arab-Israeli Yom Kippur conflict.

(3) Although there is no reliable hard data on this, all main sources agree that the first phase of the war in Ukraine produced more casualties among the armed forces than among civilians. The exact opposite occurred in the outbreak of the war in BiH, that is, when the greatest number of the total estimated 40,000 civilian casualties of the conflict occurred.

Unprecedented Aid in the War in Ukraine

Taken by surprise by the fact that the threatened Russian military invasion had actually become a reality, the main Western Bilateral Actors quickly developed a common position of firm and harsh condemnation of Moscow and unconditional defense of Kyiv's sovereignty. Remaining indirectly involved in the conflict, they immediately converged on the need to send wide-ranging aid to Ukraine, moving as donors on the ground almost in real time with the outbreak of war (Trebesch et al., 2023; Szőke and Kolos, 2023; Grossi and Vakulenko, 2023; Bosse, 2022; Dräger, Gründler and Potrafke, 2022; Hashimova, 2022; Republic of Poland Donors' Conference, 2022).

The same actors present in the pre-war geo-political and diplomatic context mobilized, i.e., bilateral (from the US to the UK; from France to Germany) and multilateral institutions (mainly NATO and the EU). Western actors that in the Bosnian scenario had remained passive and long undecided about the scope and degree of their involvement on the field entered Ukraine with decisive and radically opposite narratives, timing, types of reaction, and assistance compared to those shown earlier in the Western Balkans. Only a few days after the start of the invasion, Kyiv became the recipient of an intense and in many ways unprecedented aid campaign, whose contents and objectives were much more extensive than those recorded not only in BiH but in most other recent war scenarios (Ibid.). The level of geo-political contention and state actors involved extended the scope of aid far beyond humanitarian intervention, becoming one of the main factors influencing the events of the outbreak; this forged sufficiently effective Ukrainian military resistance to face the Russian invasion.

In this general framework, the comparison with the Bosnian case has facilitated our identification of eight directly interconnected aid policy peculiarities (Pellicciari, 2022b: 61–78). Herein, for the sake of clarity, those exceptional features have been divided into three groups: actors on the ground, the type of aid provided, or the strategic approach adopted.

Donor–Recipient Peculiarities

(1) *Response speed of Western Bilateral Donors*. At the time of the outbreak of war in Ukraine, Western Bilateral Donors abandoned the reticence to intervene that had characterized their behavior during the Bosnian case. They immediately converged on the common political and operational strategy of acting directly on the ground, moving autonomously in the provision of strong support to Ukraine (Trebesch et al., 2023; Szőke and Kolos, 2023; Grossi and Vakulenko, 2022; Bosse, 2022; Dräger, Gründler and Potrafke, 2022; Hashimova, 2022).

(2) *Leading role and primacy of Western Bilateral Donors*. A clear primacy and leading role of Western Bilateral Donors existed in defining the framework, content, rules of engagement, and aid narratives. They marginalized non-governmental actors and multilateral agencies that had been involved in operations during the Bosnian war. Furthermore, aid was openly inspired by an interventionist approach the primary focus of which was to repel the Russian invasion; humanitarian action was relegated to the background.

(3) *The Recipient-Partner*. Western Bilateral Donors had a single state recipient (the Ukrainian government) that was treated as an equal partner on the political and operational level. The latter was highly involved in the *ex-ante* co-definition and *ex-post* co-management/implementation of Western aid, and decisively influenced its composition, flow, and tactical objectives (Ibid.).

Aid Peculiarities

(1) *Quantity and diversification of aid.* Enormous diversification of aid has taken place in Ukraine, primarily concentrated within new areas of intervention in the financial, political-institutional, and military sectors; this situation is unprecedented for the beginning stages of a war. The aforesaid have far exceeded humanitarian aid in terms of resources allocated, objectives, and nature of the political debate (Ibid.).

(2) *Aid turned into hybrid weapons.* By deciding to invade Ukraine militarily, Russia resoundingly renounced the role of Re-emerging Donor on which it had spent considerable resources and efforts in the previous two decades (Bakalova, Spanger and Neumann, 2013). On the aid front, the main consequence concerned raw materials and natural resources, which Russia had traditionally placed at the center of its aid policies. By implementing a strategy that has globally restricted access to these essential commodities (mainly in the energy and agri-business sectors), Moscow has turned them into a hybrid weapon. Moreover, by exerting pressure internationally, this strategy has been used to consolidate its military position and war tactics in Ukraine (Tsygankov, 2016; Pellicciari, 2022b).

(3) *Weapons as primary aid.* In contrast to past wartime interstate aid practices, Western Bilateral Donors have openly prioritized military aid, officially placing it at the top of all aid interventions. The provision of armaments was the largest item of spending in Western support for Ukraine, far exceeding the resources allocated for humanitarian and emergency aid.

Peculiarities in the Strategic Approach Adopted

(1) *Premature opening of the post-conflict phase.* Western donors brought forward unusual political decisions for a war in its early stages. Above all (a) the acceleration of the process for Ukraine's accession to the EU, expressly granted as a sign of political support; suspending assessment of the level of transposition and enforcement of the *EU acquis* into the Ukrainian legal system; (b) an extremely early launch of the planning stage for the country's post-conflict reconstruction process,

towards which the donors' attention was strongly directed. This further diverted them from humanitarian aid.
(2) *Sanctions as aid.* Systematic, integrated use of sanctions against Moscow and aid to Kyiv took place. The sanctions were coordinated to pursue tactical objectives in the conflict and were continually adjusted and re-adjusted; subsequently the latter were quickly phased into *ad hoc* measures, in joint consultation with the Ukrainian side. The imposition of sanctions on the enemy has thus become a different type of aid to one's *Recipient–Partner.*

Neutralist Aid vs Interventionist Aid

Among the many elements that emerged from the comparison between the Aid in the Ukrainian war in 2022 and the Bosnian outbreak in 1992, two historical-political conclusions stand out which are useful for the purposes of the present work.

The first relates to the two specific case studies and confirms that, on both occasions, and although donor states reacted in opposite ways, they were mainly conditioned by foreign policy choices made according to the characteristics of the intervention scenario (Morgenthau, 1962; Furia, 2015; Hall, 2006; Wight; 1978).

In the context of the Bosnian conflict, which was foreign to the donor states and harbored an uncertain geo-political outcome, they prevaricated at length about whether and how to intervene to put an end to the war. Moreover they provided almost exclusively multilateral humanitarian aid that explicitly excluded military aid to Sarajevo (the aggressed party) even though Serbia (the aggressor) was not a nuclear superpower (O'Ballance, 1995; Burg and Shoup, 1999; Gilbert, 2016; Hill, 2011; Dahlman and Tuathail, 2005, pp. 569–99).

In Ukraine, on the other hand, Western Bilateral Donors had been present long before the conflict and had a very well-defined and deep-rooted geo-political interest in the area which was openly challenged by the Russian military invasion. They immediately intervened with their own direct presence in the crisis scenario with an unprecedented deployment of aid, giving Kyiv (the aggressed party) wide-ranging and strong support that was mainly aimed at militarily opposing Moscow to stop its advance; this, despite Russia (the aggressor) being a nuclear power (Kissinger, 2014; Dreyer and Popescu, 2014; Korhonen, Simola and Solanko, 2018).

The second conclusion is more general and identifies two different intervention models based on the differing approaches followed by the donor in the cases above.

In the Bosnian case, the war was dominated by *Neutralist Aid* implemented by specialized multilateral donors and nongovernmental actors who acted directly in the field; they were financially supported by Western Bilateral Donors who focused on external involvement at the political-diplomatic level (Dahlman and Tuathail, 2005: 569–99; Hansen, 2006; Hill, 2011).

Neutralist Aid intervened almost exclusively with humanitarian support to cover basic needs, often of the civilian population; it was apolitical, did not take sides, and aimed to limit the consequences of the war while waiting for a diplomatic solution to end the conflict.

In the Ukrainian case, on the other hand, the war featured *Interventionist Aid* characterized by an unprecedented mix of political and technical peculiarities that made its approach exactly opposite to the neutralist one. The political and operational primacy in the scenario was that of bilateral donors, who acted directly in the field with considerable aid and wide-ranging interventions.

Unlike *Neutralist Aid*, *Interventionist Aid* participated directly in the crisis with the aim of influencing its course and outcome; not only strategic but also tactical objectives were pursued on a priority basis, i.e., before humanitarian objectives. *Interventionist Aid* furthermore adapted its strategies and tactical targets to developments in the war scenario.

The two main expressions of *Interventionist Aid* that have developed separately and in an uncoordinated manner, and indeed actually colliding with one another, were the Russian *Weaponization of Aid*, i.e. the use as hybrid weapons of traditional goods donated as aid, and the Western *Aidization of weapons*, i.e., the prioritization of wide-ranging military aid in support of a single governmental recipient treated as a political partner and actively involved in the process of co-defining and co-managing aid.

From the general perspective of international relations, it can be said that Russia's foreign policy decision to switch from the use of the *carrot* (classic aid) to the *cannon* (military attack) created a war scenario in which, alongside armies, new *Aidization of Weapons* and *Weaponization of Aid* practices would also clash. The common interventionist approach that characterized this marked their dominance over neutralist and humanitarian-style Foreign Aid interventions in war zones.

5 Peculiarities of Interventionist Aid

The First Peculiarity: Response Speed of Western Bilateral Donors

The immediate and determined reaction of Western Donor States at the beginning of the war was chronologically the first of the aid peculiarities to manifest itself in the new war scenario (Trebesch et al., 2022; Bosse, 2022; Dräger, Gründler and Potrafke, 2022; Mills, 2022; Hashimova, 2022). BiH of the 1990s was completely unknown on the international stage, and outside powers intervened there for the first time, i.e., were taking a leap in the dark. On the contrary, Ukraine was well-known to the donor community, with previously established political and technical aspects guaranteeing speed of action on the ground. As stated previously, many of the Western Bilateral Donors had already been present in Ukraine for decades due to the articulated and continuous aid interventions already outlined herein; these began with Kyiv gaining independence and with aid intensifying after the Maidan revolution in 2014 (Galus, 2020).

These were a substantial number of programs which, even when they made use of external contractors, were managed directly by Western Bilateral Donors (in particular the EU and USAID) and required their presence on site, i.e., a strengthening of their field offices in Ukraine. (Bosse, 2022; Dräger, Gründler and Potrafke, 2022; Pishchikova, 2010; Woehrel, 2014). This circumstance meant that, although surprised by the outbreak of war, these donors were not unprepared to operate in the scenario therein from day one. Rather they were obliged to readjust their activities in Ukraine

DOI: 10.4324/9781003382157-5

Table 5.1 The Eight Peculiarities of Interventionist Aid

	Peculiarities	Main related issues
Actors (Donors Recipient)	Response speed of Western Bilateral Donors	Politically Motivated Aid Unprecedented Reaction
	Western Bilateral Donors Leading Role	Primacy of Interventionism (over neutralism)
	The Recipient-Partner	Recipient-Driven Aid
Aid	Aid Quantity and Diversification	Ineffectiveness and value of dispersed\diverted aid.
	Weaponization of Aid	End of Russia's Re-emerging Donor Strategy End of Russia's Multilateral Politics. Food as a Weapon
	Aidization of Weapons	Weak Legitimation of Military Aid Priorities Self-defense equated to a primary humanitarian need, i.e., a fundamental human right.
Strategic Approach	Anticipated opening of the post-conflict phase	Donor Competition over Reconstruction EU Standards vs *Political Support*
	Sanctions turned into Aid (*Aidization of Sanctions*)	Recipient-Driven Sanctions Rule of Law vs Tactical War Needs

according to the new circumstances and conditions. They had first-hand knowledge of the complex Ukrainian geo-political and political-institutional context as well as familiarity in working with its main political and administrative actors, both at the central and local level. Added to this was the importance of being able to rely on functioning and up-to-date logistical and organizational networks set up during the course of aid programs, led by team staff already in place (Trebesch et al., 2022; Bosse, 2022; Hashimova, 2022).

It was also crucial to be able to refer to a local political context that was already known and consolidated, organically structured, and hierarchically recognizable, so as to avoid the serious problems encountered in BiH in having to identify *ex novo* interlocutors in an unknown, divided, and unstable scenario that local counterparts had struggled to control. Existing operators continued to interface with the Ukrainian institutional level, with which they had enjoyed long-standing political and technical cooperation. Thus, the latter aid campaign started with the important advantage of already having a single recipient that was placed in and representative of the public sector (Dahlman, Tuathail, 2005: 569–99; Hansen, 2006). On the general political level, the main factor that enabled the immediate mobilization of the donors was a clear legitimization of their mandate to intervene decisively and unitedly in favor of Kyiv. This was the result of a common political stance among Western Bilateral actors, and one developed in the years leading up to the conflict; these actors considered and dealt with the Kyiv government as a *de facto* exclusive partner.

A relevant aspect to the above is that, in 2022, a shared vision of the geo-political framework in Ukraine allowed the actors to work with rare speed. Conversely, in 1992, the identical protagonists had been undecided on which actions to take, i.e., blocked as they were by divergent Western opinions and interests on the future of BiH and the unknown factor of the extreme weakness of the government in Sarajevo which was formally recognized but at the same time treated with distrust.

The Issue of Politically Motivated Aid for An Unprecedented Reaction

The exceptionality of the fast and determined reaction of Western Bilateral Donors raises the central question as to why it occurred in the Ukrainian case and not in other similar scenarios in the past, including BiH. The narratives of Western institutional communication portraying donor states as exclusively motivated by a desire to assist Ukraine – the victim of an invasion – were of relative value given the extent to which those interventions departed from past behavior.

As the wars in the Western Balkans demonstrated, preceding situations featuring blatant violation of a country's sovereignty followed by urgent humanitarian need, the whole of which stemmed from a political crisis, had not in other contexts resulted in similarly lightning-fast intervention to that seen in Ukraine. Therefore, the factor that prompted donor states to act in the latter case must be sought beyond the moral categories of a "just-response-to-a-right-need" of the recipient (Gilbert, 2016: 717–29; Pickering, 2014: 31–43). In fact, the pre-existing relationships that the donors had with the crisis scenario helped observers understand *how* it was possible to implement quick intervention, but not *why* this was decided upon. A possible answer can be found by looking at the donors' action from the perspective of the realist assumption that inter-state aid is conceived of and utilized primarily as a tool to defend the national interests of those who finance it (Morgenthau, 1962; Pellicciari, 2022a; Furia, 2015; Hall, 2006; Wight; 1978).

In this case, the motivation of the donor states to carry out an intervention with decidedly high costs and political risks was in the *Big Game* morphology of the Ukrainian context, the geopolitical weight of which, as seen, was significantly higher than that of BiH in 1992 (Masters, 2022; Mills, 2022). The materialization of the real possibility that Moscow might regain control over Ukraine through flash military action followed by a regime change represented the serious and concrete risk of taking Ukraine out of the western sphere of influence. Ukraine was already a solid partner as well as a key member in the western network, central to containing the growing expansion of Russian foreign policy.

From this perspective, the mere prevention of Russian expansion represented a sufficiently strong utilitarian motive to intervene in defense of a valuable geopolitical asset. It meant that, contrary to their institutional narratives, donors had decided in this case to provide massive assistance to a country primarily because of its strategic importance and much less because it was the victim of an overt humanitarian crisis or because the principle of sovereignty had clearly been violated (O'Meara, 2022; Sayapin, 2022; Cavandoli and Wilson, 2022).

A quick confirmation of the realistic hypothesis was provided by the behavior of Western Donors themselves towards Ukraine less than a year before the outbreak of the war, i.e., when the country was still amid a pandemic crisis.

At that time, neither Brussels nor Washington followed up on Kyiv's appeals for the provision of Western vaccines to cope with the country's severe health emergency. NATO was not even approached by Ukraine during the pandemic; in any case it had not proposed to play a role in the provision of aid or the management of the pandemic.

For the reasons recalled at the beginning of this book, the 2021 pandemic crisis in Ukraine did not arouse the same level of alarm in Western donors as did the Russian military invasion shortly afterwards (Pellicciari, 2021; Dräger, Gründler and Potrafke et al., 2022; Chohan, 2021).

Thus, the weaker Western reaction in the Balkans or more recently in the South Caucasus region, particularly during the Russian-Georgian war, reinforces the realistic hypothesis of aid being given to Kyiv for strategic reasons, rather than in reaction to a blatant violation of international law (O'Meara, 2022; Sayapin, 2022; Cavandoli and Wilson, 2022).

The Second Peculiarity: Leading Role and Primacy of Western Bilateral Donors

The second peculiarity of the Ukrainian context was a direct and logical consequence of the first.

The timing of their reaction meant that Western Bilateral Donors were also the first providers of aid to operate in the crisis scenario, thus accruing primacy in the field, which was unusual for a war outbreak; normally the latter is driven by other actors specializing in humanitarian aid. Not surprisingly, donors from the non-governmental and multilateral sector agencies, which had led aid in BiH at the beginning of the conflict, arrived in Ukraine after the donor states; unlike the latter, they did not have their own pre-existing structures in place. In fact, since the late 1990s, i.e., at the time of the severe post-Soviet economic and social crisis, Ukraine had no longer needed humanitarian intervention to cover its basic needs and no longer had an organized and continuous presence of specialized humanitarian workers in the field. When new widespread humanitarian needs emerged in the country, as was the case with assistance to displaced persons after the Crimean crisis in 2014, they were handled directly by donor states, primarily USAID.

The undisputed technical primacy that donor states had accrued when war broke out had empowered them to impose a characterizing imprint on the overall *rationale* behind the architecture of the aid system, namely one that delimited its scope and reflected a political range made up of geo-political sets of objectives. The latter were even more important than humanitarian aims. On the other hand, if in BIH aid had been associated with a neutral message with respect to the war, in Ukraine the message was openly under the banner of interventionism, siding with one of the parties in the conflict. Indeed, Ukraine enjoyed the status of strategic partner to the Western donors even before the conflict began.

From the Bosnian conflict in which an impartial and a-political "Aid-for-peace" message prevailed we moved to an "Aid-for-defense" treatment for the Ukrainians; the Western donors' general objective was to keep Kyiv in their sphere of influence, while their specific objective remained repelling the Russian military invasion. For donor states, the call for aid *interventionism* paved the way towards choices and strategies that ran counter to those associated with historical cases such as BiH, in which aid *neutralism* was predominant. From the perspective of the type of aid rendered, the ground was prepared for the justification of an unprecedented diversification and planning of interventions for the outbreak of a war. This fact will remain a pivotal aspect on which the remaining peculiarities of the Ukrainian case are based (Trebesch et al., 2023; Szőke and Kolos, 2023; Grossi and Vakulenko, 2022; Bosse, 2022; Dräger, Gründler and Potrafke, 2022; Hashimova, 2022).

At the very beginning of the crisis, imposing geo-political objectives on aid and broadening the spectrum of interventions beyond the humanitarian sphere resulted in a progressive functional marginalization of the importance of specialized classical donors; their prominence and visibility were thus reduced, compared to their status during other war scenarios in which they enjoyed primacy of action. Multilateral specialized agencies, primarily those orbiting the United Nations, saw the operational space available to them shrinking, given their delay in arriving on the ground; further implicated was the decrease in funding allocated by donor states who decided to act directly in Ukraine). As concerns the non-governmental sector it found itself in the unusual and difficult position of having to adapt to the timing and content of interventionist narratives that were far removed from its tradition, as well as following different rules of engagement from those to which it was accustomed.

Foremost among these was the prohibition to interact with any recipient other than Ukraine (the invaded country), even on an exclusively humanitarian level, i.e., dealing with civilian victims of war. These rules imposed total closure towards Russia (the invading country). This aspect was one of the radically opposite rules compared to those predominant in the Western Balkans, in which neutralism, in the name of the a-political nature of civilian victims of the conflict, had led to operations in all countries involved in the crisis, albeit with varying degrees of intensity. While in the Western Balkans UN specialist multilateral agencies and the non-governmental sector had intervened both in the interest of the aggressed country (BiH) and the country considered to be the aggressor (Serbia), in the Ukrainian conflict both Western donors and Russia raised insurmountable obstacles to any multilateral humanitarian cross-country initiatives aiming to assist particular categories of war victims, such as Ukrainian refugees who fled to Russian territory when the war broke out.

The Issue of the Primacy of Interventionism

Central to this were the implications of a wartime scenario where the prominence of donor states put them in a position in which they defined the approach and key words of the overall aid framework for the recipient. If moving to defend a national interest was part of classic state behavior in foreign policy, this happening in a war in which donor states predominated was a (partial) novelty that ended up conditioning and dictating rules of engagement and narratives for the entire aid system. *Interventionism* made a quantum leap in Ukraine, going from a foreign policy strategy to a paradigmatic reference value for all actors and the entire aid system (Olsson, 2015: 425–41; Morgenthau, 1962; Pellicciari, 2022a; Furia, 2015; Hall, 2006; Wight; 1978).

The bottom line is that in doing so, the idea of *Neutralist Aid* was abruptly set aside; what was once a solid point of reference for Western donors which had, in previous decades, inspired the framework for emergency humanitarian interventions that characterized aid in the main war scenarios, was now simply incompatible with the geo-political context of the moment. Although in the first months of the war this circumstance went unnoticed in the overexcited chronicles accompanying events, the replacement of *neutrality* by *interventionism* created a new benchmark in the evolution of aid policies between states. In essence, the conditions were created for state-funded aid that prioritized strategic objectives linked to the course of the war over coverage of the basic needs of war victims. It was a turning point for aid policies given that the practical consequences determined in the manner in which we understand priorities for action in a war, the type of activities to be undertaken, the financial resources to be allocated, and the institutional narratives to be channeled to frame the aid intervention for the domestic public opinion.

The institutionalized *modus operandi* determined an inversely proportional relationship between the political weight of the scenario and the centrality of classical interventions for civilian victims of war; the interventionist approach diverted attention and resources traditionally reserved for humanitarian aid (Ibid.). The paradox in the context described was that it was precisely because the intervention concerned a scenario of geo-political interest to the donor states that the basic needs of the civilian population took second place, especially in the phase of the outbreak in which their needs were most acute.

The Third Peculiarity: The Recipient-Partner

Confirming that Western aid should be seen primarily as a foreign policy action to help a partner country, donor states involved the Ukrainian leadership in the various phases of aid initiatives in a manner befitting an international state partner rather than a classic aid recipient. This dynamic was facilitated by the automatic transfer of the nature of the West's pre-existing political relationship with Kyiv to the aid plane, which gave it the authority and strategic importance of a partner. Contacts and negotiations during the war ran parallel to the institutional channels developed over decades of Ukrainian–Western dialogue; these intensified after the Maidan revolution in 2014. The Ukrainian leadership from that period was the only interlocutor recognized by the West in the process of defining aid to Kyiv.

What was new compared to past scenarios was the high level at which the Recipient–Partner was involved in the choice of types of assistance it would be sent. From the definition of areas of intervention to participation in the distribution of aid, Kyiv was usually consulted in advance by the donors and involved in major decisions, step-by-step. The Ukrainian Government was treated as an equal counterpart and was able to influence the decisions of the donor, which was unusual for other classical recipients of aid; all the more so in the context of a war (Trebesch et al., 2023; Szőke and Kolos, 2023; Grossi and Vakulenko, 2022; Bosse, 2022; Dräger, Gründler and Potrafke, 2022; Hashimova, 2022).

As the war continued and the strategic and political importance of maintaining Ukrainian military resistance grew, Kyiv's negotiating power in determining what aid it would receive increased to such an extent that some specific types of assistance were solicited and organized at Kyiv's initiative and involved explicit, autonomous requests. That Ukraine's international status and diplomatic influence continued to grow despite (or perhaps because of) its unenviable status as a country that had suffered a military invasion was reflected by the fact that that – after President Zelensky – the second most visible government figure was the Minister of Foreign Affairs, Dmytro Kuleba. To him fell the role of primary spokesman for the government's positions, not only on the composition of aid but also on purely military matters. Thus, Kuleba emerged as the front-line interlocutor with the West, surpassing the Minister of Defense, the top military hierarchies, or even Prime Minister Denys Shmyhal himself. The latter – despite being in office from 2020 – remained in the President's shadow and almost unknown to Western media (Ibid.).

Kyiv's authority has grown hand-in-hand with its decisive role as the sole recipient of all Western aid in the war scenario.

In terms of warfare, Kyiv has had the strategic importance of being a recipient determined to fight on the ground, unlike in other contexts such as Iraq or Afghanistan, where massive military assistance did not result in any local opposition to the advance of *Daesh* and the return to power of the Taliban, respectively.

From a logistical point of view, the inevitable difficulty for foreign operators to act on a field of war made Kyiv an irreplaceable partner in the co-management of aid, particularly in its implementation phase.

From a political point of view, being the only *sine-qua-non* interlocutor for any foreign intervention put Kyiv in the position of determining the order of importance of incoming aid, becoming in absolute fact the arbiter of the competition among Western Bilateral Donors for a privileged relationship with the Ukrainian government.

One indicator of the level of growth in the Ukrainian partner–recipient's legitimacy and political authority was the positive media coverage and international prestige enjoyed by Western leaders on their official missions to Kyiv; these were unusually numerous compared to other capitals of war-torn countries.

In this regard, the importance of accessibility to the capital Kyiv from outside of the city should be underlined. Despite periodic Russian missile attacks, for much of the first 14 months after war broke out it was possible for Kyiv to be reached by foreign leaders over land. In turn, those journeys became political messages, such as the arrival on the same train by Mario Draghi, Emmanuel Macron and Olaf Scholz in June 2022. Similar, and extremely symbolic, was the visit to Kyiv by the US President Joe Biden, one year after the start of the war (February 20, 2023).

Returning to the comparison of Ukraine with the Western Balkans, it is no coincidence that one of the elements that had contributed to weakening the authority of the Bosnian government and further complicated the war context was the extreme difficulty experienced by travelers entering and leaving the besieged capital of Sarajevo. The latter had to wait until the end of the war to receive the first official visit of an American president, i.e., Bill Clinton's meeting with the Bosnian Collective Presidency, on December 22, 1997.

The Issue of Recipient-Driven Aid

The high and unprecedented level of involvement of Kyiv's government in the definition of aid translated into an equally unprecedented ability to influence the structure and orient the management thereof.

This repeatedly contradicted one of the main trends of interstate aid policies in recent decades, starting precisely with the post-conflict scenarios in the Western Balkans. Namely they were largely the result of Donor-Driven Processes, with recipients seemingly involved in important roles but, in reality, are subordinated to accepting interventions largely decided and managed by the donor.

As the conflict in Ukraine continued, Kyiv's ability to politically affect Western donor choices reached levels far greater than in the pre-war period. Before the conflict, although firmly in the Western camp, Kyiv had been more exposed to the paternalism of Western partners/donors and subjected to the merciless assessments, severe criticism, and stringent recommendations regarding policies to be followed and reforms to be adopted (Ibid.).

The Western aid narrative in 2022 conferred positive international visibility on Ukraine, along with an aura of legitimacy that rendered it immune to criticism. The result was a strengthening of Kyiv's political authority as a recipient of aid, as well as its ability to relate to donors on an equal footing. However, this presented donors with the delicate question of how to deal with and manage the recipient's growth in autonomy, particularly when a shift occurred from traditional Donor-Driven dynamics to Recipient-Driven ones, i.e., when the local counterpart gained sufficient authority to publicly exert political pressure on donors for particular types of aid; moreover, uncoordinated public appeals to Partners occurred. An example of this was when the donors were clearly put in a difficult position by pressing Ukrainian demands for further military and financial aid; on some occasions, the latter were even expressed in harsh tones. First and foremost, this was done by the Ukrainian President, who had a high media profile echoing his every statement. This was best demonstrated by the case of the Leopard 2 tanks that Berlin decided to supply to Kyiv in January 2023, yielding to Ukrainian and US pressure.

In that case contributing to overcoming the German government's reticence was the very visibility of Kyiv's public appeals in this regard; the latter shone a spotlight on an issue generally treated with the utmost secrecy in the defense sector, thrusting that question into the arena of parliamentary political debate. It was a deliberate and effective communication strategy adopted by Kyiv that aimed to back German Chancellor Olaf Scholz into a corner. In April 2022 this was also the case when Ukraine resoundingly refused to welcome German President Steinmeier's visit to Kyiv. All the while, in a doorstep statement on April 7, 2022, while attending a meeting of NATO foreign ministers in Brussels, Minister Kuleba publicly urged Germany to provide more and faster weapons. He made that request without hesitation and stated that the Ukrainian agenda was very simple and consisted of only three points: "weapons, weapons and weapons".[1] Similar demands made in the media in the form of urgent but stern public appeals to Western leaders punctuated the entire period at the beginning of the war. Such public pleas intensified as the months went by, gaining visibility when Zelensky or Kuleba attended meetings of the leading Western multilateral institutions either in person or remotely. Just one year after the diplomatic incident recounted above, Germany announced a €2.7 billion military aid package for Ukraine, ahead of Zelensky's visit to Berlin.

These attitudes were indicators of a political authority of the recipient that was bound to increase as the war continued, and had become a rather frequent political element; indeed, the donors themselves, in their mutual competition to render aid to Ukraine, found it difficult to manage and contain the recipients' autonomous calling attention to themselves in public communications (Morgenthau, 1962; Pellicciari, 2022a; Furia, 2015; Hall, 2006; Wight; 1978).

This aid dynamic underscored the inconsistency of a rather widespread belief in the Western media that portrayed the Kyiv government, even during the war, as a mere executor of Western decisions, particularly those of Washington. However, in moving from classic recipient to Recipient-Partner, the Ukrainian government had, in fact, demonstrated an autonomy not seen in earlier Donor-Driven intervention scenarios, from BiH, to Kosovo, to Afghanistan. The respective political leaderships of these countries had always followed the directions advocated to them by the donors, taking care not to challenge them publicly (Dahlman and Tuathail, 2005: 569–99; Hansen, 2006).

Thus, two other rather widespread publicist beliefs regarding the conflict in Ukraine must be relativized, namely that (a) the arms supply and (b) the end of hostilities depended *solely* on the will of the Western Bilateral Donors, ignoring the active influence exercised by the Recipient-Partner on the fate and duration of the conflict.

The Ukrainian President's mission to the US in December 2022 and his European tour in May 2023 best showed how Ukrainian political authority had grown since the beginning of the war. During his visit to Washington, President Zelensky displayed a greater and more incisive political confidence than the low, grey profile shown by other leaders of crisis countries that had been receiving US aid, best exemplified by late visits to Washington by Afghanistan's President Hamid Karzai.[2]

During this European tour, designed to show that Kyiv was not a mere executor of decisions imposed from outside, emerged the obvious political difficulty that some of the donors, notably Italy, had in making the Ukrainian President's open demands for more armaments compatible with the domestic narrative of Rome and the Vatican in favor of negotiating a peaceful solution to the conflict.

The Fourth Peculiarity: Quantity and Diversification of Aid

A consequence of the leading role of Western Bilateral Donors was also the peculiarity of the exceptional amount of different types of aid channeled to Ukraine at the beginning of the war. Since the end of February 2022, primarily on behalf of the US, UK, EU, and NATO's bilateral and multilateral initiative, there has been a continuous succession of announcements of new aid allocations, often communicated in person by Western leaders during their missions to Kyiv, as mentioned above (Trebesch et al., 2023; Bosse, 2022; Dräger, Gründler and Potrafke, 2022; Mills, 2022; Hashimova, 2022).

The purely quantitative aspect of this flow was less surprising than the qualitative one. The greater financial resources structurally available upstream to the public sector in donor countries, and the facilitated procedures for direct expenditure that could be activated in emergency situations, created conditions for the deployment of an impressive volume of aid that would otherwise be difficult to achieve in classic non-governmental and multilateral interventions. Overall, aid dimension exacerbated the usual difficulties in accurately recoding interventions in war zones, as well as in obtaining disaggregated data on aid actually delivered. As opposed to aid that had only been announced for political reasons but was yet to be delivered (Ibid.).

As was the case in other war scenes, poor, last-minute decision-making plagued the initial period, coupled with faulty planning and scarce operational coordination between the donors, despite their political convergence regarding the Ukrainian scenario. Rather, what clearly marked the Ukrainian case was the variety of interventions, starting with the unconventional type as opposed to the traditional aid commonly given during the outbreak of a war. The level of diversification in the aid expressed the strong political value and geo-political aims of Western Bilateral Donor interventionism, going so far as to involve sectors and assets unrelated to the predominant humanitarian interventions witnessed in war contexts (Ibid.).

What stood out was the repeated use, in a highly unstable context, and without any particular adaptation, of aid mechanisms that traditionally have been applied to stable countries that had reached an advanced stage of their democratic transition. This was the case with the exceptional macro financial assistance used to send transfers of financial resources directly to Kyiv to support the considerable running costs of the state's political-administrative institutions; these transfers were in the context of a war economy that had dramatically impacted domestic tax revenues. With unusual rapidity compared to the slowness shown in the past, both towards Ukraine and in the management of direct financial aid, the European Union deliberated, and above all disbursed to the Ukrainian government, exceptional MFAs in the amount of €1 billion in August 2022 and a further €5 billion between October and December 2022. Added to that was €1.2 billion of the sixth MFA, paid in March 2022. The aforesaid amounts were in addition to an allocation of MFA €18 billion that was set for the following year, of which €4.5 billion was disbursed by March 2023 (Ibid.).

These were very substantial framework interventions that were gradually joined in continuous cascade fashion by interventions by individual bilateral donors for smaller amounts to meet emergencies and needs that accrued during the conflict. However, as the war continued, the main component of Western aid consisted of military assistance to enhance the equipment and capabilities of the Ukrainian army.

In addition to the fundamental Ukrainian determination to resist militarily, in the context of this book, it is no exaggeration to emphasize that it was the exceptional Western aid provided to Kyiv that made it possible to contain the Russian invasion.

The largest donor in the military field was the United States with €32.5 billion in aid given in the first year of the conflict alone, compared to only €700 million spent in the previous year. Meanwhile in the same period the EU, through its European

Peace Facility (EPF) – a financial instrument outside the EU budget that has been operational since July 2021 – had committed €3.6 billion in military assistance for Ukraine. That financing included lethal equipment (€3.1 billion) and non-lethal supplies (€380 million).[3] In addition to the many arms supplies that were repeatedly announced and relaunched in the media, military aid to Ukraine included a wide range of interventions which remained shrouded in secrecy due to their tactical importance in the ongoing conflict (Ibid.). These ranged from strategic advice given to the Ukrainian military leadership on how to conduct the war, i.e., to support intelligence and counter-intelligence activities, to the transfer of the technological know-how needed to use the new weaponry, to the capacity-building activities of specific army departments for special operations. As confirmed at the start of the conflict by NATO Secretary General Jens Stoltenberg himself, it should be emphasized that some of this military aid was a direct continuation of military assistance programs to and in Kyiv that were already underway well before the war (notably by the US, UK and Canada), namely as early as 2014 (Bosse, 2022; Dräger, Gründler and Potrafke, 2022; Pishchikova, 2010; Woehrel, 2014).

As the armed clash continued, and as it became evident that the conflict would not be as short-lived as initially assumed by most, the types of military assistance intensified, entailing more articulated interventions with medium-term impact. The supply of more sophisticated armaments by the Western donor countries was accompanied by prolonged periods of technical training for the large units of the Ukrainian army assigned to operate them (e.g., 90 soldiers just to operate a single Patriot missile battery). As a direct expression of the interventionist approach military aid soon occupied the stage of Western action in Ukraine, relegating the classic humanitarian aid of war scenarios to the background. This reduced visibility was also matched by a consequent reduction in the resources allocated by donor states for all the interventions that did not have a direct strategic impact on the course of the conflict; in the first year of the conflict, the EU allocated €668 million for humanitarian aid programs to help civilians affected by the war, of which as much as €630 million was given directly to Ukraine.

This was happening at a time when, conversely, even other budget items were being diverted to military expenditure, introduced to deal with other emergencies, such as the pandemic; as for example when Internal Market Commissioner Thierry Breton, in following up the European Council's decision to supply Ukraine with at least 1 million munitions a year, proposed to authorize Member States to also draw on the post-pandemic EU Recovery Fund allocations for this purpose.[4]

Military aid had become so prominent in the political debate that it had also been evoked as the first response to basic needs aggravated by the prolonged conflict; for example, even when faced with the prospect of a harsh winter without sufficient electricity and heating, the first calls for aid were for the reinforcement of Kyiv's anti-aircraft defense system instead of the supply of generators (Trebesch et al., 2023; Bosse, 2022; Mills, 2022; Hashimova, 2022).

Again, the opposite was true in the Western Balkan context where, in BiH, humanitarian interventions were long unchallenged at the center of the inter-state aid agenda while almost four years had passed before a Western military intervention (which was, moreover, rather simple and quickly implemented) ended the bombing of Sarajevo and the longest siege in the history of warfare at the end of the twentieth century (Dahlman, Tuathail, 2005: 569–99; Hansen, 2006).

The Issue of the Ineffectiveness and Value of Dispersed Aid

The main issue related to such a broad spectrum of aid concerned the problems of its implementation during a war. The level of deconstruction, instability, constant change and, of course, danger to personal safety have traditionally made the war scenario one of the most difficult contexts in which to operate (even more so at the time of the outbreak). The supply of aid during a war has always been *sui generis* in form and content; this activity features unpredictable variables that, for donors, are unique among aid scenarios, reserved for specific types of assistance that would require the definition of special rules of engagement.

In most previous war scenarios, providing aid had mainly been a matter of interventions that, in response to the need to act quickly in changing contexts, i.e., to respond to sudden and unforeseeable basic needs. Many of the latter would be direct, circumscribed, and deliberately unsophisticated humanitarian interventions, with a logic of "quick impact" rather than "quality of implementation". Typically, such operations would have been deliberated, financed, and implemented with simplified administrative procedures for reporting, procurement, and auditing. In turn, these difficult operating conditions had justified the creation of a specific category of donors and implementing agencies to support them, who specialized in the distribution of aid in particular emergency crises.

The presence of such a different operating logic had been behind the decision to keep the agencies and offices responsible for humanitarian aid separate inside the same international organizations as those responsible for development cooperation aid (such as ECHO and EuropeAid in the EU, or UNHCR and UNDP within the UN).

Aid provided in major crisis situations has traditionally been subject to serious distortions that have undermined its effectiveness. Considered inevitable and physiological, efforts have been made over time to keep them within acceptable levels by fragmenting aid into a multiplicity of basic, quick-impact humanitarian actions supported by simple logistics.

On the contrary, in the case of Ukraine, a dangerous short-circuit was created when those in an uncertain and unstable neo-war context were obliged to host an enormous amount and variety of aid, i.e., the kind generally designed for more structured post-crisis transition scenarios. Naturally the highest value by default of that aid was subject to monitoring and formal and substantial audit and control procedures (Crawford and Bryce, 2003: 363–73; Gilbert, 2016: 717–29; Pickering, 2014: 31–43).

On the one hand, the instability following the war aggravated the risk of classic phenomena such as the overlap of aid, the lack of coordination between donors, the impossibility of carrying out accurate track record of the interventions, and the dispersion of aid linked to inefficiency and logistical problems (Crawford and Bryce, 2003; Trebesch et al., 2022; Bosse, 2022; Mills, 2022; Hashimova, 2022). On the other hand, military and financial aid with a much higher financial value than humanitarian aid was granted without conditionality, controls, or monitoring, in open derogation of what had previously been planned and adopted by the donors themselves.

For example, in authorizing the May 20, 2022 payment of €600 million to complete the Emergency MFA deliberated before the start of the war, a *force majeure* call went out for a suspension not of the ongoing macro-assistance (as per practice) but of the conditionalities placed upfront on the recipient that were required to proceed with the disbursement. Even more surprising was that such a completely non-traditional and administratively questionable decision was officially announced:

> the outbreak of the war impeded the capacity of the Ukrainian state to implement the limited set of structural policy measures associated with the second instalment of the assistance. The Commission decided, nevertheless, to disburse the second instalment (…) given that the fulfilment of the conditionality had been impeded by force majeure, which the Member States endorsed.[5]

The increase in the resources allocated for aid in the face of reduced donor control in their management by a recipient with known problems of corruption in public administration has stimulated episodes of misappropriation the arbitrary and deviant use of resources, and conflicts of interest. Needless to say, the same physiological rate of dispersion of aid during war, when applied to sophisticated and very expensive technological armaments rather than to food supplies and basic necessities, has raised the risk that substantial funds might be diverted in far greater amounts than in the past.

Quite a different issue and systemic impact on the crisis was posed by the possibility of 100 sacks of rice "going missing" in a typical humanitarian aid intervention, rather than by the disappearance of same number of portable anti-tank missiles costing USD 250,000 per unit (such as the FGM-148 Javelin, provided by the US to Ukraine since the beginning of the war).[6] Western concerns in the first year of the war included the growing suspicion that some of the military supplies sent to Kyiv were at the root of the global surge in the black market for arms that had coincided with the Ukrainian conflict.[7]

All the while, in Kyiv, civil servants and government officials at the highest levels were being removed from their posts because they were suspected of corruption and embezzlement of resources allocated to the army, as in the striking case in January 2023 involving deputy head of the Ukrainian presidential office Kyrylo Tymoshenko, four deputy ministers, and five governors.[8]

The Fifth Peculiarity: Aid Turned into Hybrid Weapons (Weaponization of Aid)

Within a framework of novelties almost exclusively attributable to the actions of Western Bilateral Donors, Moscow in turn contributed to the evolution (or involution, depending on one's point of view) of the political use of aid. This emerged not so much from a comparison with the Bosnian case of 1992, in which Russia played a very marginal role in the first, dark post-Soviet decade, but from observing the historical evolution of Moscow's aid policies in the first two decades of Vladimir Putin's legacy at the helm of the country (Dahlman and Tuathail, 2005: 569–99; Hansen, 2006). From this perspective, the military invasion of Ukraine marked a surprising break with Russian aid policies with respect to the post-Soviet period, and a radical change in the use of the main assets of those policies.

In resorting to a military option to assert its geo-political interests, Russia went in the opposite direction to the West; the latter, albeit driven by the same motives, nevertheless responded by intensifying its aid policies, i.e., primarily diverting them to unconventional areas such as military aid (Larionova et al., 2016; Brezhneva, Ukhova, 2013; Yushkov, Oding and Savulkin, 2017; Gray, 2015: 273–88). In a move that surprised most observers, Russia renounced the "aid + diplomacy" pairing that had inspired its foreign policy on several occasions since Moscow emerged from of the shadow of being a recipient of Western post-Soviet assistance in the 1990s to becoming a donor itself on a global scale in what had been an attempt to improve its international status. On the other hand, by opting for a military option in Ukraine, Moscow renounced its role as Re-Emerging Donor and nullified the considerable efforts it had made in the previous period to accredit itself in this regard.

At the multilateral level, in the two decades preceding the war, Russia had ensured active participation and substantial financial contributions to missions and aid programs of major international organizations. At the bilateral level, it had considerably increased the network of third countries that received its aid, borrowing from the Soviet period the practice of explicit, direct links between foreign policy and state aid; similarly, it adopted the USSR's catch-all aid concept involving assistance in the most diverse sectors (starting with the provision of natural resources on extremely favorable conditions).

Compared to the West, Russian aid differed in its frank geo-political objectives, exhibited with something approaching pride. Aiming simply at the political obligation of the recipient, Moscow never tied its aid to the conditionalities often demanded by Western donors. It was an approach to aid to which Moscow remained faithful up until the Covid-19 crisis: in the first phase of the virus outbreak, by sending medical assistance to third countries (such as the "From Russia with Love" mission organized in Italy) and by distributing the Sputnik V vaccine according to purely political-diplomatic criteria and channels, Russia demonstrated its disdain for the market logic imposed in the West, i.e., the economic-commercial vaccines developed in private hands (Pellicciari, 2022a; Fidler, 2020; Chohan, 2021).

The year 2022 thus marked a complete reversal of Russia's *modus operandi* as Re-emerging Donor. As previously recalled herein, Moscow had extensively played the latter role during the decades of its "Aid War" waged against Western donors; indeed, Ukraine itself had long been a beneficiary of that policy. From an operational point of view, the main structural change concerned the approach put into practice by Russia towards the very assets that had traditionally been used in the name of catch-all-Aid, starting with natural resources and raw materials. From goods granted on favorable terms, these became an offensive instrument in which Moscow selectively limited its global distribution following the logic of geo-political interests. This was conducted regardless of the cost for the state budget of the latter, unlike the US approach. This process, described as "Weaponization of Aid", was undertaken/pursued by Russia systematically in response to the introduction of Western sanctions, making it not only a political but also a tactical asset to be used by default in concrete international disputes.

As is natural, in addition to the hydrocarbon sector, other less visible but equally important sectors of assistance existed to which the same approach was extended, involving a long list of raw materials of which Russia remained the world's leading exporter. These were indispensable to produce key commodities on a global scale (Götz, Glauben, Brümmer, 2013, pp. 214–26). Such was the case of the agri-food sector, where access to grain and fertilizers, as well as the movement thereof, was unblocked in alternating stages; the methodology of these negotiations was reminiscent of the exchange of prisoners during wartime.

In synchronizing the Weaponization of Aid with the evolution of the Ukrainian conflict, Russia has made it a tactical hybrid weapon for its openly declared geo-political purposes. Alluding to the conclusions of this book, it should be noted that Russia has openly treated the Weaponization of Aid as a war tactic, without feeling the need to ideally link it to the country's previous role as an international Re-Emerging Donor. As stated earlier, the latter vanished with Russia's military invasion of Ukraine.

That Moscow considered practices like the *Weaponization of Aid* to be legitimate expressions of its realist foreign policy, i.e., to be used in this manner when necessary, was best summed up by Russian Foreign Minister Sergey Lavrov's lapidary comment to the BBC in June 2022: "Russia is what it is. We are not ashamed to show who we are".[9]

The Issue of Aid Turned into a Hybrid Weapon

The use of natural resources and raw materials as a pure tactical asset of war was a direct result of Russia's decision to switch from the use of aid to the use of tanks in foreign policy. This was a circumstance that many feared before the war, but few thought would actually happen.

The related issues to be highlighted here are of a general nature and concern the impact that the sudden disappearance of that the role of Russian as a Re-emerging Donor had on the tradition of state-funded aid in international relations in the 2000s (Larionova et al., 2016; Brezhneva, Ukhova, 2013; Yushkov, Oding, Savulkin, 2017; Gray, 2015, pp. 273–88).

Russia's Divorce from Multilateral Cooperation. A domino effect occurred in Russian diplomatic closures vis-à-vis the West in areas not directly related to the ongoing military campaign in Ukraine. Thus, a further shift took place in the actions of the former, i.e., from the classic multilateral level to the bilateral one. The aforesaid followed a trend that had already begun in 2014, thereby reversing the multilateral cooperation policies adopted by post-Soviet Russia in its first two decades. In the name of its military invasion, the Kremlin has stopped or reduced cooperation and exchange in areas where, in recent years, the resources given had exceeded those received (Larionova et al., 2016; Brezhneva, Ukhova, 2013; Yushkov, Oding, Savulkin, 2017; Gray, 2015, pp. 273–88). This ranged from the discontinuation of international missions in the Arctic, to a reduction of cooperation in space, and continued with Russia's quitting the Bologna Process Higher Education System, to its resounding final abandonment of the Council of Europe as well as the European Court of Human Rights (Allison, 2013; Gould-Davies, 2020, pp. 7–28).

These choices represented a breaking off of decades-long relations that foreshadowed a prelude to a long-term disengagement by Russia from aid and cooperation policies with the West; they represented something akin to a lengthy divorce rather than a temporary separation (Karaganov, 2022: 50–67, Lukyanov, 2023: 5–10).

Food as a Weapon. Added to the serious global repercussions of these strategies is the enormous symbolic impact represented by the involvement of wheat in the hybrid war in Ukraine. In addition to being an indispensable commodity for the social and political stability of entire areas of the planet, wheat has been the commodity with which humankind – over the last century – came to identify with the very idea of "food": the concept of nutrition summarized in a single commodity. Solidly at the center of emergency and humanitarian aid since the end of World War II, wheat has been the image *par excellence* of development cooperation, to the extent that it inspired the emblem and motto (*Fiat Panis* – let there be bread) of one of the oldest existing international organizations, and the first one established with the aim of combating hunger in the world – the Food and Agriculture Organization of the United Nations (FAO).

The repeated use of wheat as a legitimate, hybrid, but conventional weapon in the increasing geopolitical competition worldwide marked a break with classic aid policies that had an impact equal to the recognition of military assistance as a legitimate form of aid. This triggered a new phase in which aid policies became part of the War; in this era the normalized use of food as a weapon and of weapons as a primary form of aid also clashed.

The Sixth Peculiarity: Weapons as Primary Aid (Aidization of Weapons)

The way in which Western countries presented the variety of their aid interventions in Ukraine marked a political turning point in the previous practice of international state aid in war contexts.

This was particularly true in the face of the centrality assumed by military aid, i.e. by types of assistance that were far from the traditional perception of aid in an emergency situation of a conflict. In the past "aid" was something rooted in common sense and sustained by decades of past institutional narratives about State Foreign Aid being "good" because it was humanitarian and a political. Even more so when it was set in a wartime context (Trebesch et al., 2023; Szőke and Kolos, 2023; Grossi and Vakulenko, 2022; Bosse, 2022; Dräger, Gründler and Potrafke, 2022; Hashimova, 2022).

With surprising ease, interventions in areas such as the military (which are generally difficult to justify to the emotionally shaken public in the face of war) have been openly placed on top of Foreign Aid interventions since war broke out in Ukraine.

In Western institutional communication, initiatives such as armament supplies were referred to in the same tones reserved for traditional emergency and humanitarian aid, thus associating them with the categories of necessity, urgency, and a just cause for intervention. It went against the political-institutional practice since the end of World War II, in which international military aid was considered a legitimate part of Foreign Aid in peacetime; particularly when used multilaterally for conflict prevention, peacekeeping and stabilization in post-conflict contexts (Allison, 2013).

On the contrary, before Ukraine, military bilateral cooperation between states implying transfers of technology or the direct supply of armaments or strategic support, had required it to be carried out behind the scenes, especially in wartime contexts; indeed, the discretion required in those transactions nearly bordered on state secrecy. The same lack of visibility has applied to the military aid given for highly strategic purposes, as requested by the secrecy surrounding the aforementioned NATO aid to Ukraine, ongoing since 2014.

After decades, this distinction has disappeared in the Ukrainian case, promoting an aid campaign in a war emergency in which military assistance was openly put at the top of the inter-state aid list, thereby institutionalizing a practice that is defined here by the neologism of "Aidization of Weapons".

The latter was given great visibility and simply put in place with no explanation provided. As the war dragged on into a conflict of attrition, the osmosis between aid policies and military support became stronger, with accounts of arms shipments being reported in the media with far more attention than humanitarian aid initiatives for the Ukrainian population.

Throughout the period of the war observed here, this remained the orientation of the Western Bilateral Donors, who were divided over which and how many armaments to send, without questioning the principle of the primacy of military aid,

Simply the latter was presented as "legitimate insofar as it was just" and "fair insofar as it was necessary". Again, given the similar premises and the involvement of the same-state actors active in Ukraine, a comparison with the Bosnian conflict speaks of radically opposed narratives and political choices.

At the outbreak of the war in BiH, despite the very high number of civilian casualties, Western bilateral aid sent to Sarajevo was humanitarian and had excluded the supply of armaments, even for a defensive purposes, i.e., to free that besieged city (Dahlman and Tuathail, 2005: 569–99; Hansen, 2006). The donors had invoked the same neutralism put into practice by the international military contingents of UN blue helmets mobilized during the conflict as interposition forces between the parties, with limited engagement protocols that prevented them from participating in the conflict, even if in defense of the civilian population, as in the Srebrenica massacre that occurred despite the presence of Dutch blue helmets. Among the arguments that were used at the time to justify the refusal to give military assistance to Sarajevo was that doing so would be siding with one of the warring parties, even if it was the one being attacked, thus fueling the conflict. Thirty years later, the same aid narratives were adopted by the same donors to justify actions in Ukraine that were the opposite of those that had been taken in BiH.

The Issue of Prioritizing Military Aid in War

Although Western infotainment, institutional communication, and political debate have not dealt with it, the official predominance given to aid in the unconventional form of the Defense sector was among the main peculiarities of the Ukrainian case, and the one with the greatest potential implications for the future (Estrada et al., 2022; Mills, 2022).

If military assistance granted to a partner under attack for geopolitical reasons was a recurring situation in international relations, the surprising novelty of the Ukrainian scenario was not only the enormous scale of this assistance, but also the high visibility given to it, in a clear effort to legitimize its priority status over other aid, including humanitarian interventions.

Unlike the military assistance programs that the West had already provided to Kyiv, the new context required the need for popular legitimization in the face of the prospect of the huge resources that needed to be allocated to cope with the new scenario; furthermore, the predictable heavy impact on the socio-economic situation in the donor countries also needed to be framed adequately Trebesch et al., 2023; Szőke and Kolos, 2023; Grossi and Vakulenko, 2022; Bosse, 2022; Dräger, Gründler and Potrafke, 2022; Hashimova, 2022).

Given that all political leaders indiscriminately suffered a decline in popularity due to their handling of Covid-19 and, furthermore, that the consequences of the pandemic itself had already frayed and stressed social contexts, Western donors avoided using geopolitical categories to justify a massive intervention in Ukraine in the eyes of their public. Such costly military assistance in a war threatened to become an accelerator of an upcoming economic recession.

Hence the donors' attempt to morally legitimize military aid, i.e., by emphasizing the criteria of its necessity and urgency, as well as representing ethical justice in the Ukrainian context. For this reason, it was necessary to present military aid not as an alternative to other "good" humanitarian aid interventions, but ideally as constituting the very essence of virtuous intervention (Masters, 2022; Mills, 2022).

The point Is that this path of legitimizing the supply of arms within the framework of *Interventionist Aid* was simply put into practice based on a political decision in the moment, without changing the old aid narratives; this, even though, traditionally, activities such as hardcore military cooperation were rarely juxtaposed with classic Foreign Aid activities, or at least not publicly.

Under the pressure and the tight timeframe imposed by reacting to the unexpected Russian military attack, this attempt to morally legitimize aid in the eyes of one's domestic public opinion resorted almost exclusively to the classic emotional narratives of Foreign Aid. In the brutality of the Ukrainian warfront, the donor states inevitably and visibly fell into obvious logical contradictions and conceptual potholes.

For the Western donor states, the main risk associated with legitimizing *sic et simpliciter* interventionist military aid, according to the old Foreign Aid categories, was that it facilitated the introduction of new principles in international relations; nevertheless, in other future contexts, these could backfire on them.

An example of this was the Ukrainian war itself, when Russia took advantage of the historical precedent of a political solution introduced by an act of force; paradoxically that cited had been carried out by the US in 2003. Thus, in justifying the decision to invade Ukraine, Moscow presented it as making a defensive move by referring to the same controversial principle of "preventive intervention"[10] invoked by Washington in Iraq during the second Gulf War (Roberts, 2022: 22(2); Crawford, 2015:12–18; Levy, 2011: 87–96; Karaganov, 2022: 50–67). That political decision had been denounced by many at the time as a dangerous conceptual leap that could harbor unpredictable future consequences, precisely because it could easily be applied to other contexts.

Another example was given by the implications of having declared military assistance a priority at a time of clear emergency (the beginning of the war). The consequence, far from being theoretical, has been that the right to self-defense has been equated in all intents and purposes to a classic primary need for survival; it follows that fundamental human rights and armaments have been put on the same level as primary humanitarian aid, identical to food and shelter.

Looking ahead, this represented the indirect introduction to another fundamental principle that is potentially quite problematic, precisely because of its inherent contradictions and the weakness with which it has been defined: namely, the creation of a framework of justification in crisis scenarios for the allocation of resources to supply arms rather than humanitarian aid (Masters, 2022; Mills, 2022).

The Seventh Peculiarity: Premature Opening of the Post-conflict Phase

Facilitated by the climate of great attention and the widespread feeling of solidarity created in Western countries, many among the numerous national and international actions in support of Ukraine, were of a political-institutional nature and were promoted directly by the donor states themselves (Trebesch et al., 2023; Szőke and Kolos, 2023; Grossi and Vakulenko, 2022; Bosse, 2022; Dräger, Gründler and Potrafke, 2022; Mills, 2022; Hashimova, 2022). Some were characterized by the timing with which themes were introduced at the moment of the outbreak of the war, while in other past contexts they had appeared near to or following the cessation of hostilities. The surprising peculiarity of the Ukrainian case was the very early stage at which the donor states launched a series of initiatives more in keeping with a post-conflict transition phase. These actions were inspired by the same interventionist spirit as the aid, i.e., to send a clear political signal about the long-term future of Western support for Ukraine.

Firstly, the topic of *reconstruction* of the damage caused by the conflict was officially opened at the Donors' Conference in Warsaw on May 5, 2022, organized by the European Union in cooperation with the Polish government (Republic of Poland Donors' Conference, 2022). Alongside emergency and humanitarian interventions, which in the Ukrainian crisis meant urgent support for refugees and internally displaced persons (7.7 million internally and 5.2 million abroad), the conference initiated the programming of an initial allocation of €6 billion for the reconstruction of Ukraine's infrastructure and economic system. Although the emergency aspects of the humanitarian crisis engaged much of the work of the conference, this announcement of post-conflict appropriations was enough to trigger a strong interest in this matter in Western government circles.

Even before the summer of 2022, several countries had organized ad hoc bilateral technical–political missions to Kyiv to discuss post-conflict interventions with the Ukrainian government, openly bidding to take a leading role in reconstruction. In the circles associated with public enterprises and leading industrial trade organizations in Western countries, the main theme soon became the opportunities expected for managing the reconstruction of Ukraine's infrastructure. As the months passed, the issue of reconstruction grew even stronger and, together with the issue of military supplies, dictated the international agenda. In fact, it contributed to a further reduction in attention and interest in humanitarian aid.

In the second half of 2022, despite complications in the conflict and an increase in uncertainty concerning its duration and outcome, the importance of the reconstruction theme increased to such an extent that it dominated the three subsequent Donors' Conferences rganized within the space of a few months; first in Lugano (July 4 and 5, 2022), Berlin (October 25, 2022), and Paris (December 13, 2022). The fact that the approach to reconstruction was political rather than technical was clearly stated in the premises of these appointments, for example in the document from the International Expert Conference on the Recovery, Reconstruction and Modernization of Ukraine in Berlin. The aforesaid declared that the goal of the event was fully political, namely to demonstrate "… unwavering support from the EU and the international community to Ukraine in the face of Russia's unprovoked and unjustified war of aggression…".

Even more surprising, considering the EU's previous track record, was the early establishment (January 23, 2023) of a *Multi-Agency Donor Coordination Platform to support Ukraine's Repair, Recovery and Reconstruction Process,* the stated aim of which was to "ensure enhanced coordination amongst all key players providing short-term financial support but also longer-term assistance for the reconstruction phase". The institutionalization of a structure for managing and directing post-conflict aid only 11 months after the outbreak of war was one of the most striking differences in the approach adopted in the Western Balkans. In the latter, the corresponding institution, i.e., the European Agency for Reconstruction (EAR), was only set up in 2000, after all the conflicts in the area had ended. Furthermore, it was not made clear whether and how the platform created in Ukraine intended to avoid the problems of (a lack of) transparency encountered in the Western Balkans, namely in the mixed public-private management of very significant funds (particularly in the procurement and tendering procedures) that contributed to the very non-ritual decision to completely dismantle EAR in December 2008 (Pellicciari, 2022a; Ramboll report, 2009).

Similar dynamics in the war involving the politically motivated anticipation of post-conflict institutional plans were present in the topics surrounding Euro-Ukrainian integration. As previously described, those plans were among Kyiv's top priorities in the pre-conflict period, yet it was stingy in terms of concrete results. The war unblocked a stand-off that since 1994 had seen Ukraine aspiring to draw closer to the EU and repeatedly asking to join; meanwhile, although Brussels intensified cooperation with Kyiv, it had, in reality, avoided defining the formal steps of incorporating Ukraine into the European Union. To justify lengthening the accession process, the EU had repeatedly emphasized Ukraine's shortcomings in adapting to the EU *acquis* as well as the endemic unresolved political-institutional and socio-economic problems of its democratic transition. The latter were still largely incomplete according to the very same EU assessments on the results of the assistance it rendered to Ukraine (Bélanger, 2022; Sapir, 2022: 213–17).

Since the first days of the Russian invasion, political statements had been made from many quarters in the West in favor of Kyiv's accelerated and, in some cases even immediate, European Union membership. In the proponents' own words, this was a reaction to Moscow's invasion conceived of as compensation to Kyiv for the Russian invasion it had suffered; furthermore, it constituted a *de facto* incentive to continue opposing that violation. As in the case of the reconstruction issue, the potential acceleration of the EU accession process was associated with the dynamics of the war and disconnected from the country's progress in legislative harmonization and political-institutional reforms and from an assessment of Ukraine's level of compliance with the strict standards required to become a full Member State of the European Union.

Due to the interventionist climate that had been created, these appeals were not treated with the same skepticism that had been reserved for those who had called for Sarajevo and Zagreb to join the European Economic Community (EEC) in 1992; again those pro-European calls were made in the belief that a move towards integration into the EEC would have greatly limited the escalation of the war. That Ukraine's acceleration towards EU membership was intended to represent political support was demonstrated by the meager space reserved in the media for technical comments. Again, the latter pointed out the Ukrainian delay in the EU *acquis* process, and the length of the technical-administrative paths to EU membership, which were ill-suited to the timing of war narratives. As a result of the mounting pressure, and as a compromise solution, on June 22, 2022 the European Council granted Ukraine the coveted and long-desired status of *Candidate Country*, for the first time officially shifting the question from "if" to "when" Ukraine would become an EU Member State (Ibid.).

On this point, the comparison with the Western Balkans underlines another blatant political divergence in the choices made by Brussels in accepting new Member States into the Union. In the early years of the Bosnian post-war transition, i.e., following the Dayton Peace Accords, donors were slow to move from a humanitarian emergency state to reconstruction issues. In general, the fact that the individual states of the former Yugoslavia had been the theater of war resoundingly slowed down their path to EU membership. With the exclusion of Slovenia (which joined the EU in 2004) and Croatia (a Member State since 2013), the rest of the republics that emerged from the break-up of Yugoslavia have remained stuck in the time loop of the European integration process; their EU hopes have been slow in coming to fruition. BiH, despite having an effective population of less than 3 million and having emerged from the war for nearly three decades, in 2022 was still firmly under international protectorate, which effectively kept Sarajevo's EU accession an unrealistic and unrealizable prospect.

The Issue of Donors Competition over Reconstruction

Acceleration on the issue of post-conflict reconstruction and Kyiv's path to EU membership raised a number of both political and technical questions that were in both cases related to aid initiatives being purely political and far too premature in nature.

The obvious technical problem with consideration of reconstruction in Ukraine as early as May 2022 lay in the impossibility of quantifying resources and planning interventions based on a framework of needs that was still completely unknown. Suffice it to say that during 2022, the greatest infrastructural damage in Ukraine, i.e., the kind that reconstruction aid is primarily aimed to remedy, occurred over six months after the first Donors' Conference kicked off on the subject (Republic of Poland, Donors' Conference for Ukraine, 2022; Trebesch et al., 2023).

Pre-planning reconstruction was a technically risky move taken at a time when it was clear that the conflict would continue, but not for how long; moreover, and, in particular, beyond the proclamations made by the warring parties, it was not clear whether the post-war configuration of Ukraine's territory would remain as it was before the Russian invasion.

This was not an insignificant fact, continuing to bear in mind that the major destruction on which reconstruction would have to intervene involved precisely the areas in which Ukraine's territory is disputed, i.e., the part which Moscow claimed as part of its Federation. It was unclear if and when they would return under the control of the government in Kyiv.

From the point of view of relations among donors the political question was even more insidious.

If talk of repairing the war damage served to evoke a positive wartime epilogue for Kyiv and project an optimistic image for the future, the side effect was the triggering of a premature rush among Western bilateral actors to be protagonists in the reconstruction, attracted as they were by the substantial political and economic benefits guaranteed by its management. As a result, at a time when the war was still in its early phase, donors were distracted from the humanitarian issues of the present and began to position themselves with an eye to their future prospects, competing with each other according to dynamics already seen elsewhere, from BiH, to Afghanistan, to Kosovo (Annen and Moers, 2012; Dahlman and Tuathail, 2005: 569–99; Hansen, 2006; Hill, 2011).

Moreover, it was worrying that a level of management for reconstruction aid was established so far in advance, without shared assessment of the considerable problems that had marked previous decades of aid programs in Ukraine, as well as in almost all other key-intervention scenarios. Planning aid in future post-war Ukraine without taking into account the inefficiencies of the past was indicative of a careless disregard for replicating the mistakes and financial waste already witnessed in other scenarios. Donors' attention was entirely focused on high expectations from participating in the management of the future reconstruction phase, deliberately wiping out memory of the problems encountered in their same aid programs to Kyiv in the three decades before the war (Trebesch et al., 2022; Bosse, 2022; Dräger, Gründler and Potrafke, 2022; Mills, 2022; Hashimova, 2022).

Almost a year after Warsaw, the conference in Rome in April of 2023 was a brief flash in the parable of the reconstruction plan; the event principally moved the topic of reconstruction from constituting assistance to Ukraine to representing a golden opportunity to boost donors' economies. The Conference had been strongly sought by the new Italian Prime Minister Giorgia Meloni, who, unlike her predecessor Mario Draghi, was made to suffer politically by Paris and Berlin for having been less involved in direct European relations with the Ukrainian Government.

Organized as a separate event from the others already held on the topic, the Rome Conference was essentially an opportunity for a host of Italian business-oriented companies and economic operators to try to develop privileged, one-on-one relations with their Ukrainian counterparts. It was more of a lobbying event than a planning event for future reconstruction.

Returning to the subject of the strategic role of the *Recipient-Partner*, the Italian Conference reports an episode indicating how Kyiv made skillful political use of being the *sine-qua-non* interlocutor for multiple Western donors competing in the race for post-war reconstruction.

In an interview with the Italian press one month before the event, Foreign Minister Kuleba implied that donors' military aid and their future involvement in Ukrainian reconstruction were linked:

> Those in Italy who talk about peace and not weapons want Ukraine to cease to exist (...) Ukraine will be the biggest building site in Europe (...) Italian companies could be involved and make healthy profits.[11]

The Issue of EU Standards vs Political Support

Regarding the promotion of Ukraine as an EU candidate country, the short-circuit between the political issue and the technical aspects was equally glaring in its simplicity. Obtaining candidate country status irrespective of the completion of the planned, mandatory transposition of important European standards into its national legislation proved to be a political stretch; not surprisingly, criticism arose over the fact that the enlargement process constituted the milestone of the legitimacy and sustainability of European integration. The decision to shortlist Ukraine for EU candidacy again brought up the question of the evaluation criteria followed by Brussels, underscoring how parameters thought to be objective and universal were, in reality, applied unevenly and bent to the political needs of the moment.

Staying on the road to accession, the issue of the arbitrary judgment with which Brussels had, on other occasions, assessed the compliance of candidate countries arose once more: from the generous exceptions granted in the "premature" enlargement of the EU to Romania and Bulgaria in 2007, to the rigidity shown more recently in the Serbian and Georgian cases.

The uneven application of European parameters again led to obvious paradoxes, such as in March 2023, when Brussels denied Tbilisi candidate country status for insufficient progress in judicial reform and anti-corruption simultaneous to the visit of the President of the European Parliament, Roberta Metsola to Ukraine. While visiting Kyiv the latter praised the speed of Ukraine's process to EU membership, despite EU assessment reports stating that the country's pre-war domestic situation was worse than that of Georgia, particularly present in the justice and anti-corruption sectors.[12] Such a critical framework could not have improved in a war context that was, by definition, unsuitable for real institutional reform processes, as demonstrated by the sensational arrest of Vsevolod Knyazev, the Head of the Ukrainian Supreme Court in May 2023; the Justice was investigated along with 18 other judges and accused of having taken bribes in the millions.[13] Moreover, even accepting that the war was reason enough to bring Kyiv closer to the EU, it was unclear why the same reasoning had not been applied to Tbilisi; years before Ukraine, after a conflict with Russia, the latter had lost control over Abkhasia and South Ossetia, i.e., territories the sovereignty of which is Georgian according to the EU and NATO.

Under the pressure that developed due to the new war scenario, the European Commission was accused of exhibiting arbitrary behavior in the different attitudes adopted towards some of the Member States of the so-called Visegrad group, the members of which had engaged in bitter clashes with Brussels (Bélanger, 2022; Sapir, 2022: 213–17). Upon the outbreak of war in Ukraine, after being accused of nothing less than denying the basic European principles of a rule of law, Poland – strongly supporting Kyiv and opposing Moscow – was pardoned *de facto* and ceased to be a target of criticism from Brussels. Conversely, the latter continued to profess a position of intransigence towards Hungary, in what was read in diplomatic circles as retaliation for the Hungarian President Viktor Oban's explicit criticism of the EU's policy of closure towards Moscow.[14]

The Eighth Peculiarity: Sanctions as Aid (Aidization of Sanctions)

The last of the particularities identified herein concern a new type of approach to sanctions and its impact on aid dynamics.

Under the impetus of the Ukrainian crisis, the sanctions have taken a further step in an astonishing evolution that has made them unexpected protagonists of international relations in the new millennium. For military purposes sanctions have traditionally been conceived of as a kind of state siege and thus have long represented a tactical "last-step-before-war", i.e., to be the preparatory antechamber of inevitable war-like denouement. However, when the bipolar international system ended, sanctions underwent a profound transformation starting in the 1990s, becoming the "first-option-alternative-to-war" in international confrontation. Easy to introduce and durable over time, they have become functional for hybrid confrontations between states while avoiding the use of weapons (Dreyer, Popescu, 2014; Korhonen, Simola and Solanko, 2018).

Set out in a category of their own among the preferred diplomatic solutions in international crisis management, the stories surrounding sanctions are ideally complemented by those aid policies, albeit the two act on separate but parallel planes. The fact that they were conceived of as tools to achieve opposite effects in a binomial relationship with the recipient meant that the use of one has often sidelined use of the other. That there has been little mutual coordination in their use is proven by the recurring situations of coexistence on the bilateral and multilateral level of "aid to enemies", as in the case of EU aid to Turkey for Syrian refugees, despite the difficult relation of the former with Ankara. Instead, an example of "sanctions to friends" was in the intensive Italian-Russian cooperation that took place until 2022, despite the EU sanctions framework; obviously Rome had to comply with the rules of the latter.

The scope of the further evolution that sanctions underwent in Ukraine has concerned their use in coordination with aid, which has gone from being occasional to systematic; the latter was facilitated by the fact that the concrete use of the two instruments has fallen under the same political-institutional direction. At the same time, the content, structure, and rules of engagement of the sanctions were changed.

It was a process that followed the same rationale applied to aid, which aimed to make sanctions a hybrid offensive instrument; dynamic, but above all subject to constant updates, to follow the tactical needs of war.

Within days of the Russian invasion, the existing Western sanctions framework which had been introduced in 2014 against Moscow, was quickly strengthened with new content and a much broader scope of impact, involving previously uninvolved sectors (Korhonen, Simola and Solanko, 2018). The EU acted by constantly supplementing its sanctions framework with new packages of measures, released monthly. One year into the war, ten such packages had been introduced by Brussels, and showed no sign of stopping.

Compared to the past, a clear intention existed to create closer links between sanctions and aid. This was demonstrated by the lively debate on the use of Russian assets that were seized in the West during 2022, which were estimated at around €330 billion (Mbah and Wasum, 2022: 144–53; Gioe and Styles, 2022; Way, 2022: 5–17).

Although it remained at the level of a mere proposal, an example of this was the European Commission's hypothesis to proceed with the definitive expropriation of Russian capital, to give it to Ukraine as a war indemnity; under that hypothesis a joint financial structure would have been created, with the Kyiv government managing its use. The intent of such restrictive measures would have targeted one side (the aggressor country) so as to directly benefit the other side (the aggressed country) in the conflict. Simply making this assumption was indicative of the level of integration on the Western side between the aid and sanctions frameworks.

Another example of the coordination between sanctions against Moscow and political aid to Kyiv was given by the International Criminal Court (ICC). In Ukraine the latter acted on a very different timeline than that of the International Criminal Tribunal for the Former Yugoslavia (ICTY) in the Western Balkans. Both these judicial bodies are UN-backed; similarly, their pre-trial inquisitorial action assumed the political value of a strong sanction for those subjected to it.

In the Bosnian case, the indictment of Slobodan Milošević and other prominent leaders took place long after their participation in the signing of the Dayton Peace Accords. Glaringly, in the case of Jadranko Prlić, indictment took place ten years after the fact, four of which he had even spent as Foreign Minister of the postwar BiH government.[15]

On the other hand, in the Ukrainian case, with the conflict still in full swing, the arrest warrant issued in March 2023 against Russian President Putin represented a censure of Russia, despite the incredibly slim chance of its being carried out. The result of that symbolic act was a strong political endorsement of Kyiv and had an equally effective impact on public opinion in the West.

Another major change from the recent past was that these sanctions, like the aid, were in practice decided together with the Ukrainian counterpart, i.e., the aid recipient itself. In a crescendo during the first months of the war, Kyiv was involved *a priori* by Western bilateral donors in defining not only the aid to be provided to Ukraine but also strategic restrictive measures to be imposed on Moscow in crucial sectors such as energy (Trebesch et al., 2023; Bosse, 2022; Dräger, Gründler and Potrafke, 2022; Pishchikova, 2010; Woehrel, 2014).

This was another significant difference with what had happened in past scenarios such as BiH; in the latter case, the international community had not consulted Sarajevo in the restrictions decided against Serbia, and had kept aid to the former separate from the sanctions on the latter; they were harsh, but yet disconnected from the everyday life on the Bosnian front (Dahlman and Tuathail, 2005: 569–599; Hansen, 2006; Hill, 2011).

Used as a weapon under the direction of the aid Recipient-Partner and in a circumstance in which armaments were elevated to a legitimate form of aid, an "Aidization of Sanctions" process was completed, indicating how sanctions (against the enemy) had become a systematic and powerful form of aid (to the partner).

The Issue of Recipient-Driven Sanctions

Along with Kyiv's involvement in the shaping of sanctions against Moscow, the issue of a Recipient-Partner not always politically attuned to donors' expectations came up again. This was another side effect of the exponential growth in international authority of the Ukrainian counterpart after the first months of the war. Kyiv found itself in the unprecedented position of being able to put political pressure on Western bilateral actors regarding the kind of restrictive measures it believed should be taken against Moscow.

This was done without sparing public criticism of the measures considered insufficient or not in line with Ukrainian expectations, as in the case of the introduction by the EU/G7 coalition of a price cap on seaborne Russian oil products, considered too mild; likewise weak (according to Ukraine's leadership) was Europe's answer to the calls for greater restrictions on the travel of Russian citizens to Western countries.

Due to the significant growth in *status* and international sympathy for Ukraine, the Western leadership could not react to this criticism with the same tone. Such a swift change in the dynamics of political dialogue would have been unthinkable only a few months before the outbreak of war, i.e. when it was the West that was criticizing and Kyiv justifying itself. The result was that, as the war continued, Recipient-Driven processes were not limited to the field of aid policies alone but became a more frequent dynamic in the concrete definition of sanctions as well.

The Issue of Rule of Law Principles vs Tactical Needs

In the frequent use made of sanctions as a tactical measure, much of the sacred imagery related to it has been compromised, i.e., solemn punishment imposed exceptionally by the International Community against those responsible for a blatant violation of International Law. The new approach led to continuous changes in technical aspects such as the mechanisms and resolutions adopted to implement the restrictive measures, with no justification given other than their importance to achieving the tactical objectives of the moment.

However, this led the sanctions of the West to the paradox of introducing, or even justifying, measures that openly contradicted some of the founding principles of that same liberal-democratic culture in the name of which the donors had justified their use against Russia in the first place (Dreyer and Popescu, 2014; Korhonen, Simola and Solanko, 2018). The most controversial case concerned the numerous restrictions of civil rights for Russians introduced by Western countries against all individuals, indiscriminately identified on *the sole basis* of being citizens of the Russian Federation

In addition to the classic individual sanctions against institutional representatives and political figures responsible for or directly linked to the current crisis, sanctions against the entire Russian population were added, with cascading measures in numerous sectors, from the financial field to tourism and culture. The latter have effectively rendered every Russian a *persona non grata* in the West, particularly in the first months following the outbreak of war.

However, in the West's pursuit of the tactical goal of increasing popular Russian discontent with the Kremlin and stimulating the emergence of a Russian opposition movement, it fell into the obvious paradox of applying a concept of collective responsibility that is blatantly contrary to the principle of individual responsibility.

The aforesaid underlies the Rule of Law and is one of the pillars of Western liberal-democratic constitutional and cultural identity.

In addition, some of the Russian confiscation of assets have been the subject of controversy, in particular individual confiscations that were generically switched to target "oligarchs", i.e., to a social category outside state institutions, not defined by objective criteria (Kalyanpur; 2020; Rutland, 2014:1–8). Many of these confiscation operations were conceived as political retaliation against Russia but have created serious concerns about the soundness of the legal basis on which they rest. This is especially when confiscation is carried out against persons who have often not even been charged with specific crimes by a court of law or a court order. Furthermore, adding to the feeling of arbitrarily switched measures was the exclusion of prominent figures from the lists of sanctioned oligarchs; the latter were not spared because of any particular merit, but because they were central players in the export of raw materials and natural resources vital to the Western industrial system.[16]

Again, a comparison with the Balkans in the 1990s calls the attention of observers to diametrically opposing behavior adopted by the same actors. The harsh regime of international sanctions commuted against Slobodan Milošević's Serbia had resulted in a substantial flow of Serbian citizens away from the country; yet the doors of the West were not closed against them. Accepted with visas and humanitarian residence permits, they were granted similar status and reception rights as the refugees from the former Yugoslavia who came from war-torn countries i.e., BiH and Croatia.

The wall erected against Milošević did not exclude from Western aid the Serbs who left their country during the war in BiH, as did the virtual wall indiscriminately erected against all Russian citizens. In particular, the number of Russians that have left their country to evade the Russian military mobilization called for in September 2022 is estimated to be 3 million people between the ages of 19 and 55; most of the members of this group are highly educated urban youth who can largely be assumed to be opposed to fighting in the war in Ukraine.

Notes

1 NATO News, "NATO Secretary General with the Minister of Foreign Affairs of Ukraine Dmytro Kuleba", April 7, 2022 www.youtube.com/watch?v=OWy379REwRg
2 www.youtube.com/watch?v=XGg7Ss1x7wA
3 European Commission, Service for Foreign Policy Instruments, European Peace Facility https://fpi.ec.europa.eu/what-we-do/european-peace-facility_en
4 www.agenzianova.com/en/news/ucraina-breton-gli-stati-membri-dellue-potranno-usare-i-fondi-di-coesione-e-pnrr-per-le-munizioni/ www.politico.eu/article/european-commission-unveils-plan-to-boost-eu-defense-industry/
5 (https://economy-finance.ec.europa.eu/international-economic-relations/candidate-and-neighbouring-countries/neighbouring-countries-eu/neighbourhood-countries/ukraine_en)

6 www.cbsnews.com/news/ukraine-javelins-us-100-million-security-assistance/
7 www.ft.com/content/bce78c78-b899-4dd2-b3a0-69d789b8aee8 / www.theguardian.com/world/2022/jun/02/ukraine-weapons-end-up-criminal-hands-says-interpol-chief-jurgen-stock / www.cato.org/commentary/sending-weapons-ukraine-could-have-unintended-consequences
8 www.washingtonpost.com/world/2023/01/24/ukraine-officials-ousted-corruption-zelensky/
9 www.bbc.com/news/world-europe-61825525
10 http://kremlin.ru/events/president/news/67843 Interview with S. Karaganov "Is Putin placing bets he cannot win?" on BBC HARDtalk, February 3, 2023. Available at: www.bbc.co.uk/programmes/w3ct32h4.
11 www.agenzianova.com/news/kuleba-chi-in-italia-parla-di-pace-e-non-di-armi-vuole-che-lucraina-cessi-di-esistere/
12 www.europarl.europa.eu/news/en/press-room/20220401IPR26508/roberta-metsola-backs-ukrainian-people-in-kyiv
13 https://nabu.gov.ua/en/news/nabu-sapo-expose-corruption-scheme-in-supreme-court/
14 https://ec.europa.eu/commission/presscorner/detail/en/ip_22_7273
15 www.icty.org/en/case/prlic
16 www.europarl.europa.eu/doceo/document/P-9-2022-003408_EN.html \ www.opensanctions.org/datasets/peps/

6 Interventionist Aid vs Pandemic Aid

The characteristics and peculiarities of Interventionist Aid in Ukraine define the common political ground for a comparison with Pandemic Aid, quite apart from the suggestions of a publicist narrative that *a priori* imagines them to exist in a permeable state.

However, given that their chronological overlap cannot be ignored, the comparison between Interventionist Aid and Pandemic Aid (as was already the case when dealing with the Ukrainian and Bosnian cases) is developed here on three levels: (1) the Scenario in which they are set; (2) the Actors (recipients and donors); and (3) the main structural characteristics of the assistance rendered.

Scenario: Aid as a Central Driver of International Relations

The structural differences between the two crises and their respective scenarios were mentioned at the beginning of this work. The pandemic was an unforeseeable natural catastrophe that happened overnight, at the global level; furthermore, its impact was unprecedented, at least in the contemporary age. Almost all the world's governments found themselves navigating uncharted waters and improvising virus containment measures on their own, without absolute points of reference. Meanwhile multilateral efforts were practically absent during the first year of the pandemic (Pellicciari, 2021; Fidler, 2020; Chohan, 2021). Conversely, although a surprise, the war in Ukraine was not unanticipated, though it did represent a worst-case scenario. Unlikely as it had seemed, war had, in any case, been included among possible developments. Occurring in a dramatic manner previously seen in other past contexts, the war

DOI: 10.4324/9781003382157-6

crisis directly affected a circumscribed and well-defined territory, and automatically triggered diplomatic and military protocols and instruments, both bilaterally and multilaterally (Estrada et al., 2022; Mills, 2022; Bosse, 2022; Hashimova, 2022).

However, from the perspective adopted in the present work, the main common trait of the war and pandemic crises was the absolute centrality that aid, defined in the sense of *International Aid Public* Policies (IAPPs), played in them. To the extent that it became a primary distinguishing feature and driver of the internal dynamics of the conflict, much more so than in previous cases in which aid was only *one* of the plans on which state actors related during the crisis. In both cases, IAPPs catalyzed and occupied a large part of the international relations of their time, becoming an almost exclusive diplomatic channel through which interaction between institutional actors belonging to different states was channeled with an intensity unknown in other scenarios of widespread instability in the 1990s; that is true whether one is speaking of crisis or transition dynamics.

During Covid-19 both the initial phase of medical supplies to limit the spread of the contagious virus *and* the subsequent phase of Vaccine Diplomacy dominated state relations on a global scale. Those phases were conditioned by political fallout far beyond what was *strictu sensu* their impact on the field of health. On the other hand, the Western aid sent to Ukraine in the first year of the war was so decisive that it was among the factors opposing Russian military action (Gehring, 2022; Mbah and Wasum, 2022: 144–53; Gioe and Styles, 2022). What was exceptional was that, in both crises, IAPPs directly affected the development of the scenario, playing an even more central role because they concerned contexts characterized by crises in full swing. Those dynamics contrasted with what had been seen in similar previous historical cases, i.e., where "aid-in-crisis" did not go beyond basic humanitarian and emergency interventions to mitigate its effects (Gilbert, 2016: 717–29; Pickering, 2014: 31–43).

Contrary to what the differences in their respective origins would suggest, it was the aid in the outbreak of the Ukrainian war that brought about the greatest changes in the political balance within the respective international system of reference. In fact, although the pandemic was a crisis initially caused by an a political natural event, in its continuation the politicization of aid, and vaccines in particular, developed along the lines of preexisting international relations. These confirmed the old power relations (Trebesch et al., 2023; Bosse, 2022; Dräger, Gründler and Potrafke, 2022; Pishchikova, 2010; Woehrel, 2014). Although the Eastern Geopolitical Vaccine countries (first and foremost Russia and China) moved as unchallenged donors roughly in the eight months between 2020 and 2021, as soon as the western economic-commercial vaccine countries solved the supply issues in their distribution systems, the international balance returned to the old framework of fractures, alliances, and opposition.

Conversely, although the war in Ukraine was due to human factors and featured more circumscribed territorial impact, the clash between Western aid and Russian military action triggered a redefinition of geo-political power relations of a global and long-term nature. The latter was not only limited to the duration of the conflict. A BRICS-driven Eurasian front was pitted as an emerging alternative pole to the US-driven Euro-Atlanticist Western front; surprisingly, in the midst of crisis and transition, the former was unexpectedly joined by new partnerships between states that had once opposed one another, such as Saudi Arabia, Iran, and Syria (Gehring, 2022; Krickovic and Pellicciari, 2021: 86–99; Krickovic and Sakwa, 2022; Haroche and Quencez, 2022: 73–86).

While the pandemic had raised general ontological questions about the future of mankind, it took only a few months of the war in Ukraine for it to become clear that a new world order was in the making, and who stood to be its protagonists.

Actors: Rise of the Bilateral Donor

Another aspect common to both crises was the prominence of donor states that had overshadowed non-governmental/private donors and international agencies/organizations (primarily those of the UN) that specialize in emergency crisis contexts (Hill, 2011; Pickering, 2014: 31–43; Gilbert, 2016: 717–29; Gray, 2015: 273–88). Determined to have direct operational involvement in the field, bilateral donors strongly reduced the delegation of intervention management and implementation to third parties or Implementing Agents, reversing what had been a practice in the growth of IAPPs. This resulted in the aid recipients in both crises being central government institutions in the countries affected;

those entities possessed considerable authority and steering power over the orientation and management of aid.

If anything, it is interesting to note that, in Pandemic Aid, it was the eastern geo-political vaccine bilateral donors who used the vaccine as an asset for IAPPs, while by not controlling its production and distribution, western economic-commercial vaccine countries effectively suspended their activities as donors. Thus the latter did not fulfill vaccine requests from countries that traditionally received their aid (Pellicciari, 2022a; Fidler, 2020; Chohan, 2021). The opposite happened in the Ukrainian conflict, where the roles were reversed, and the protagonists of Interventionist Aid were the Western Bilateral institutions. On the other hand, the Eastern institutions reverted to the use of military force to promote their own foreign policy; Russia with its invasion of Ukraine, and China with its unprecedented increase in defense budget spending. It was no coincidence that the latter coincided with the escalation of China's dispute with the US over the future of Taiwan.

Another common aspect of the two crises was the prevalence of bilateral donors over multilateral ones, though the intensity of that difference varied. The latter experienced one of the lowest moments of their political legitimacy and operational credibility during the pandemic. From the virus outbreak onwards, almost all aid passed through sovereign states, which acted autonomously with respect to the multilateral institutions that were unable to formulate a rapid response to the emergency. They were blocked by organizational models designed not for autonomous decision-making but for the management of administrative tasks on behalf of the Member States.

After having invested considerable resources and political commitment to re-inventing itself on the issues of global warming and ecological transition, the UN found itself completely unprepared to deal with an unforeseen pandemic-type emergency. The WHO itself, the only UN agency to enjoy initial credit for the health emergency, soon lost credibility due to a series of contradictory statements on the origin of the virus as well as recommendations on how to deal with it (Özler, 2020; Pellicciari, 2022a). On the other hand, NATO, one of the protagonists of the Ukraine crisis, was completely absent during the pandemic, to the extent that, in June 2021, on the occasion of its seventieth-anniversary celebrations, Secretary General Stoltenberg strongly underlined opposition to China and Russia as the Atlantic alliance's priorities, without making any reference to the pandemic. This though the latter was still in the emergency phase in almost all of the UN member countries (Depledge, 2021: 80–90; Haroche and Quencez, 2022: 73–86; Ringsmose, Rynning, 2021: 147–68; Schuette, 2021: 1863–81).

The EU was overruled by its individual Member States on iconic decisions such as the unilateral suspension of Schengen, while at the vaccine stage it struggled mightily to obtain the doses necessary to be redistributed internally for national immunization campaigns (Wolff and Ladi, 2020: 1025–40). It was only at the *Global Health Summit* in Rome in May 2021 that a multilateral initiative of the European Commission in the field of vaccination aid to third countries (Covax) regained momentum; even then, the event was successful due to the decisive political support given by the G20, chaired at that time by Italian Prime Minister Mario Draghi. As the former President of the European Central Bank (ECB), Draghi had maintained strong ties with EU institutions. The political predominance of bilateral over multilateral donor states was also confirmed in the Ukrainian crisis, although to a lesser extent than in the pandemic, and with different situations depending on the institutions and/or international organizations involved.

The EU and NATO clearly played a central role in the initial definition and implementation of most of the peculiarities of the Interventionist Aid from a political and military point of view respectively; however, in the long run, these institutions stood out for their role in connecting and jointly coordinating the bilateral donor states, rather than as autonomous decision-making centers in their own right.

Indeed, as the war continued the intensification and articulation of military aid and the dispatch of armaments to Ukraine further emphasized the autonomous action of Western national leaders. The latter individuals preferred to interact directly in a bilateral mode with the Kyiv government, and did not hide the any friction that developed over differences in views and operations of different national strategies (Trebesch et al., 2023; Bosse, 2022; Dräger, Gründler and Potrafke, 2022; Pishchikova, 2010; Woehrel, 2014).

The weak role played in Ukraine by the various UN-linked multilateral agencies was shown by the clear correlation between political weight and donor prominence on the ground in the Ukrainian context. Penalized by its inability to act as a mediator between the conflicting parties, the United Nations had, in fact, been relegated to the margins of diplomatic action; this, save for periodic votes on resolutions condemning the Russian invasion of Ukraine, useful in capturing the ongoing change in world balances. The latter, however, have achieved very little in concrete terms.

Aid: Weapons and Vaccines to Change the Course of Events

The political matrix and the absolute centrality they had in the development of their respective crises conditioned the configuration of Interventionist and Pandemic Aid.

Although both were accompanied by classic aid narratives that made no reference to these realist goals, they pursued very clear policy objectives using unconventional aid and novel modes of intervention (Milner in Hawkins et al., 2006).

As far as the pandemic case is concerned, *Vaccine Diplomacy* saw donors and state recipients acting based on considerations of political and economic expediency which often did not coincide with the pursuit of public health; despite the above the latter was presented to the public as the first and absolute priority for any governmental action in the face of the virus emergency (Kobayashi, Heinrich, Bryant, 2021; Pellicciari, 2021). This was the case with Russia, which, in conceiving its Sputnik V vaccine as a strategic tool for reinforcing the country's status and geo-political influence, had made the distribution of the vaccine to friendly and allied countries its number one aim, rather than making it available throughout its own domestic territory (Fidler, 2020; Chohan, 2021). Conversely, a large portion of the European Union countries that experienced severe delays in supplying the necessary doses to their populations preferred to delay their immunization campaigns rather than resorting to the Russian vaccine. Thus, they avoided accruing a political obligation towards Moscow which would have been difficult to manage in tandem with the sanctions imposed by the EU after the annexation of Crimea in 2014. This pointed to how, in early 2021, these countries actually exhibited greater political fear of the Russian vaccine than of the pandemic virus itself.

Similarly, as described earlier, at the start of the Ukrainian war, the reaction speed of Western Bilateral donors in sending predominantly military aid presented high political risks and considerable economic consequences for them; yet this became an almost inevitable choice in the face of the general objective to keep the country within the Euro-Atlantic sphere of influence by targeting the specific goal of stopping the Russian invasion (Bosse, 2022; Dräger, Gründler and Potrafke, 2022; Mills, 2022; Hashimova, 2022).

Aside from these similarities, the biggest difference between Pandemic Aid and Interventionist Aid was in their scope for change. In that sense the latter clearly prevailed over the former.

The interplay of eight peculiarities previously described here (seven referring to Western donor action and one to Russia) made Interventionist Aid an unprecedented case that can rightly be considered a radical turning point in IAPPs. In general, international pandemic aid was one-sided and was initially affected by the exceptional nature of the moment as well as the severe initial shortage of medical equipment. Later the situation was characterized by the uncertainty of the steps being taken towards Covid-19 vaccines; these depended on: research, testing, discovery, negotiation, production, distribution, and administration (Kobayashi, Heinrich, Bryant, 2021; Pellicciari, 2021; 2022a; Fidler, 2020; Chohan, 2021).

This resulted in the almost exclusive necessity for state aid in the health sector which, apart from its political importance, did not generate medium-term planning, but rather extemporaneous actions centered on the procurement of scarce assets. Other state aid in extra-healthcare fields (economic, industrial, etc.) concerned measures taken domestically rather than internationally, particularly in the economic-commercial vaccine countries. In fact, while still at an advanced stage of the pandemic, the EU expressed its prominence domestically in the massive economic-financial aid effort called the European Recovery Plan. This was aimed at its Member States rather than at international vaccine aid campaigns to third countries such as Covax (Ibid.).

In turn, the implementation of pandemic aid reverted to traditional modes of operation that were typical of health emergency contexts, i.e., relying on existing state administrations responsible for the occasion. Likewise, where appropriate, temporary *ad hoc* structures were set up. Once the acute phase of Covid-19 ended, these organizational networks were largely dismantled, leaving behind poorly institutionalized realities related to the management of pandemic aid.

Finally, an aspect described in the next chapter that was common to both crises and important for the implications relating thereto was the lack of a shared agreement between donors on the new modalities of action introduced by their respective IAPPs.

During Covid-19, Vaccine Diplomacy acted in the absence of predetermined rules of engagement, leading to a divergence of views on what the minimum requirements of Pandemic Aid should be. This led to judging the distribution of vaccines to recipient countries not by their impact on the health crisis but according to the geo-political context in which they took place, re-presenting the competition between a western economic-commercial vaccine and an eastern geo-political vaccine.

Despite, the initial severe shortage of doses, the vaccine was such a strategic resource of national interest that Western countries expressly excluded it from being sent as aid to third countries. This behavior was evidenced by the EC Implementing Regulation 2021/111 of January 29, 2021 urged by Italy, which expressly banned the shipment of vaccines outside European borders.[1]

Regarding the Ukrainian war, strong political controversies and diplomatic disputes have concerned the very practices of Weaponization of Aid and Aidization of Weapons, i.e., the main expressions of Interventionist Aid.

Throughout the period of the war considered here, Western leaders at all levels have expressed strong criticism of the Weaponization of Aid put into practice by Russia, declaring it unacceptable as a practice of war and going so far as to equate the use of wheat as a hybrid weapon with a crime against humanity.

On the other hand, during the same period, the main target of Moscow's repeated protests was the Western *Aidization of Weapons* in all its many forms, which earned the Western donors the Russian accusation of being "non-friendly countries" directly involved in the conflict. And yet it is interesting to note that the nature of the cross-party disagreement was less about the practices themselves and more about their transposition to the field of aid policies.

Table 6.1 Comparison between Interventionist Aid and Pandemic Aid

	Ukrainian Interventionist Aid	Covid-19 Pandemic Aid
Scenario	• Known type of crisis • Circumscribed war zone • Emergency crisis • Aid central driver of international rel. • Aid affects crisis development • Redefinition of international balances	• Unprecedented and unknown crisis • Global impact • Emergency crisis • Aid central driver of international rel. • Aid affects crisis development • Confirmation of old international balances
Actors		
Donors	• Bilateral Donors leading • Multilateral donors as supporting actors	• Bilateral Donors leading • Very weak Multilateral Donors
Recipients	• Single governmental recipient	• Single governmental recipient
Aid		
Structure	• Integration of policies • Multi-sectorial • Traditional aid assets • Structural peculiarities and novelties • Aimed at influencing the course of events • Non-regulated	• Temporary initiatives • Mono–sectorial • New aid assets • Not institutionalized • Aimed at influencing the course of events • Non-regulated

The fact that, in the past, the West itself has used sanctions to turn goods into hybrid weapons, and that Russia has received military aid from friendly countries such as China, India and Iran, shows that their mutual refusal to recognize that Aidization and Weaponization was not about the mechanism itself, but about the new context in which they were being used.

The Link between Aid in Ukraine and in the Pandemic

Although the crises affecting them were profoundly different, their shared political matrix underscores some important commonalities between aid in the outbreak of war in Ukraine and the pandemic.

IAPPs were a central driver of international relations.
Pandemic: Vaccine Diplomacy dominated and conditioned relations between states involved in the so-called western economic-commercial vaccine and those involved in the eastern geo-political vaccine;

Ukraine: International alliances and balances have depended on donors' decisions regarding aid for Kyiv.

IAPPs were determined to actively impact the crisis.
Pandemic: Vaccine Diplomacy has followed foreign policy *modus operandi*, pursuing geo-political interests;

Ukraine: Western Aid was the main external factor in containing the Russian military invasion.

IAPPs were wide-ranging, predominantly in unconventional areas outside of classic aid.
Pandemic: Upon the outbreak of the Covid-19 virus, aid covered emergency medical equipment, and later the various phases of vaccine management (research, testing, discovery, negotiation, production, distribution, and administration);

Ukraine: Interventionist Aid has been structurally focused on wide-ranging military and financial assistance.

IAPPs were driven and guided primarily by bilateral donors states and single governmental recipients.
Pandemic: Sovereign states acted independently, while multilateral institutions were unable to formulate a rapid response and were marginalized in the operational management of the pandemic;

Ukraine: The EU and NATO played a central role in the initial definition of Interventionist Aid. However, in the long run, their role stood out as constituting joint liaison and coordination efforts 'for bilateral donor states, rather than their being autonomous decision-making centers.

IAPPs have been largely operating in an unregulated framework, with no shared agreement among donors on the related general rules of engagement.

Pandemic: The lack of agreement on minimum vaccine standards has fueled clashes and opposing vetoes between the western economic-commercial vaccine states and those representing the eastern geo-political vaccine;

Ukraine: Western donors and Russia have respectively criticized one another over Weaponization of Aid and Aidization of Weapons practices.

Linking these findings to the results of the first comparison made here between the Ukrainian and Bosnian war contexts, the result shows a surprisingly greater proximity of Ukrainian Interventionist Aid to Pandemic Aid than to Bosnian Neutralist Aid. (O'Ballance, 1995; Burg and Shoup, 1999; Gilbert, 2016; Hill, 2011; Trebesch et al., 2023; Bosse, 2022; Dräger, Gründler and Potrafke, 2022; Pishchikova, 2010; Woehrel, 2014). At first glance, it may seem a paradox that there are more commonalities between aid in a war and aid in a health emergency than between aid in two similar contexts of war outbreaks that took place in a European geo-political space and involving the same donors. Yet, the similarities between Interventionist Aid and Pandemic Aid make sense when one considers that they took place at the same time, a full three decades after the Bosnian Neutralist Aid.

In other words, this clearly shows that the temporal distance between the historical cases of IAPPs affected their characteristics more than the morphology of the respective crises in which they operated.

Note

1 https://eur-lex.europa.eu/eli/reg_impl/2021/111/oj

7 The Interventionist Aid Revolution
Political, Conceptual, Historical

Having thus identified the historical origins, the technical-political peculiarities, and the structural innovations that characterized inter-state aid in the Ukrainian outbreak of the war, the final step addressed here is to grasp the main implications on the process of the political, conceptual, and historical evolution of IAPPs in recent decades.

The Political Dimension: New Interventionist Aid

From the political perspective of interstate aid, Interventionist Aid was the main novelty of the Ukrainian war; as stated, it was characterized by an unprecedented combination of peculiarities that nevertheless could ideally be replicated elsewhere by the donors, in other crisis scenarios of geo-political importance.

The Interventionist Aid model:

Table 7.1 The Ukrainian Interventionist Aid in the Evolution of IAPPs

Politics	• Interventionist Aid • *Success-Oriented Aid* • *Donor-Recipient Partnership* • *Recipient-Driven Aid*
Conceptual	• IAPP realist approach reinforced by three spin-offs: • *Weaponization of Aid* • *Aidization of Weapons (and Sanctions)* • *Anarchical Aid as a Key Component of War*
Historical	• The new "Interventionist Aid Phase"

DOI: 10.4324/9781003382157-7

(a) was determined to achieve strategic objectives to orient the course of events and influence the outcome of the crisis in the intervention scenario;
(b) openly placed tactical aims before humanitarian ones, with the supply of wide-ranging assistance including the provision of military and financial aid during an ongoing conflict; and
(c) featured bilateral donors active directly in the field in unmediated coordination with a single governmental recipient who – supported by its equal partner status –influenced aid programming, composition and management at both the *ex-ante* and *ex-post* stages.

While Interventionist Aid not only confirmed but even reinforced the structural intersection between IAPPs and foreign policy interests; it also presented several crucial exceptions from the IAPPs that had marked the post-war transitions in the Western Balkans and the post-soviet transitions in the former USSR (Pellicciari, 2022a; Morgenthau, 1962; Furia, 2015; Hall, 2006; Wight; 1978).

Such exceptions were related to new IAPP aspects such as: (a) Success-Oriented Aid; (b) Donor-Recipient Partnership; (c) Recipient-Driven Aid.

Success-Oriented Aid: A first major turning point of Interventionist Aid was in the special attention paid by donors to the actual achievement of the expected results of their IAPPs. Unlike the transition scenarios in the 1990s, where the simple provision of assistance was sufficient to achieve the realist objective of exerting influence on a geo-political target, in the Ukrainian crisis the interests of the donors depended directly on the effectiveness of Success-Oriented Aid. The latter aimed to achieve the objectives declared for the assistance.

The geo-political *general objective* of keeping the Recipient-Partner in the Western area of influence required that the aid delivered to Kyiv – particularly in the military and financial sector – was actually effective in achieving the *specific objective* of countering the advance of the Russian army on the ground. In other words, the effectiveness of the aid being provided was crucial to defining the donors' geo-political success in the intervention scenario. This trend was in stark contrast to the attitude of donors in the post-bipolar period; aiming to gain access to post-conflict and post-Soviet transitions, these donors had paid *more attention to the negotiation of aid with the recipients* than the effectiveness of its implementation. This, after the provision of aid had been contracted to external Implementing Agents who were mostly private, non-state actors (Pellicciari, 2022a: 110–11, 118).

Donor-Recipient Partnership vs Recipient-Driven Aid: A consequence of Success-Oriented Aid was the strengthening of a new, tighter form of political and operational interaction between Western donors and the Ukrainian Recipient-Partner. It was characterized by the active involvement of bilateral donors in the management of IAPPs in the crisis scenario, due to the marginalization of the role of multilateral organizations, the lowering of recourse to external implementing agents, and the presence of a single governmental recipient active in the aid cycle management together with (and eventually on behalf of) the donor.

In other words, Interventionist Aid pushed for an unmediated donor-recipient relationship that, compared to the past, increased the bilateral donors' sense of ownership and political control over their own IAPPs, while the Recipient-Partner saw its political authority grow. A new Donor-Recipient Partnership model emerged that was profoundly different from the transition scenarios of the 1990s; in the latter inter-state aid dynamics were heavily skewed in favor of donors at the political level, and of Implementing Agents at the operational level.

The strong and continuous connection between Western Bilateral Donors and the governmental Recipient-Partner in Kyiv has helped to preserve intact the political strength of the IAPPs, precisely because of the reduced presence of non-state Implementing Agents to mediate the relationship between the two.

In particular, being the sole recipient of all Western aid has multiplied Kyiv's strategic importance on the scenario: militarily, as the only bulwark against Russia's invasion; logistically, as an indispensable partner in the distribution of aid in the crisis scenario; and politically, as the *de facto* arbiter of the Western donors' competition in the race to position themselves in the management of future post-conflict reconstruction (Trebesch et al., 2022; Szőke and Kolos, 2023; Grossi and Vakulenko, 2023; Mills, 2022; Hashimova, 2022; Annen and Moers, 2012).

As the only authority continuously present in the war crisis field, the Recipient-Partner has developed a strong capacity to influence the strategic orientation, and concrete implementation, of aid in the field.

The influence on the composition, timing, and distribution of aid exerted by the Ukrainian Recipient-Partner concerned both the flow of armaments and financial aid provided to Kyiv as well as their intersection with the wall of Western sanctions erected against Moscow.

However, rather than weakening the donor's role, the context described above was indicative of a systematic strengthening of the Recipient-Partner, as an effect of its strategic importance in a Success-Oriented Aid context. This has resulted in an increasing number of cases of Recipient-Driven Aid, in contrast to the exclusively unidirectional nature of the Donor-Driven Aid trend present in the post-war and post-soviet transition scenarios of the 1990s.

The Conceptual Dimension: Anarchical Aid as a Key Component of War

Regarding the conceptual dimension of aid, our first considerations are methodological and concern the usefulness of the realist theoretical approach in analyzing inter-state aid; as stated previously, the latter had emerged vigorously in the Ukrainian case.

First, the realist approach made it possible to identify the early symptoms that contributed to the outbreak of war in 2022. More generally, from the perspective of a History of International Relations this analytic tool has underlined the importance of including inter-state aid among the variables defining an International System.

Second, the approach we adopted facilitated the identification of the technical-political peculiarities of aid interventions in the start of the war in Ukraine, systematizing them in the new descriptive model of Interventionist Aid.

Third, the realist perspective traced the donors' actions within their own foreign policy strategies and in accordance with precise geo-political objectives (Morgenthau, 1962; Furia, 2015; Hall, 2006; Wight; 1978).

Fourth, the IAPP concept focused on the political relationship between donor and recipient states, including any flow of inter-state assistance. This approach is best applied to the reading of aid diversity in the unconventional, wide-ranging sectors of assistance witnessed in the case of Ukraine (Trebesch et al., 2023; Bosse, 2022; Dräger, Gründler and Potrafke, 2022).

Though donors reproposed the same institutional narratives as in Neutralist Aid, the prioritization of military aid in an ongoing war has moved the current model away from the classic idea of Foreign Aid. Humanitarian aid in emergency crises and development in transition contexts had traditionally characterized the latter. Meanwhile, new realist aspects of IAPP have emerged, thanks to three spin-offs of the concept that have appeared in the Ukrainian case itself: (a) Weaponization of Aid; (b) Aidization of Weapons; (c) Anarchical Aid as a Key Component of War.

Weaponization of Aid vs Aidization of Weapons. In institutional narratives and chronicles of the Ukrainian war (difficult to distinguish from one another) discussion emerged on the *Weaponization of Aid* without providing a precise definition of its contours (Hall and Lang, 2023).

Instead, vague general references were made to the frequent intersections between assistance measures and hybrid war tactics. In reality, in the literal sense of the term, the use of aid for war purposes seemed only to apply to the Russian tactic of restricting access to key assets such as raw materials and natural resources for geo-political and military objectives.

The *Weaponization of Aid* was the direct and most obvious expression of Russia's choice to renounce the dual "diplomacy + aid" strategy that had characterized its foreign policy in the two decades before the war, particularly at the multilateral level. The Weaponization of Aid has resulted in an at-times-blatant abandonment of the entire multilateral Foreign Aid framework developed since the end of the Second World War (as in the case of Russia's exit from the Council of Europe). From a conceptual point of view, the Weaponization of Aid was one of the consequences of the hyper-realist bilateral involution of Russian foreign policy, which downgraded aid to a mere tactical asset, even when used for offensive purposes.

The Western Bilateral Donors can be placed on the same footing but in the opposite direction to Russia; they have reversed the previously existing relationship between arms and aid, rendering the former part of the latter. Placing military assistance and the supply of weapons at the top of aid policies is defined herein with the neologism of "Aidization of Weapons". This is a useful title to mark the difference between this term and the *Weaponization of Aid.*

At the same time, both concepts retain a link to Interventionist Aid. Because Western donors moved within the formal framework of classical Foreign Aid, Aidization – unlike Weaponization – has stronger conceptual implications for aid.

(1) Donors have attempted to subject military aid, and particularly that provided in a choral conflict, to a process of moral legitimacy. This was done by emphasizing the criteria of necessity, urgency, and ethical justice in military aid. The latter was presented not as an alternative to other "good" humanitarian interventions, but ideally as being at their core.
(2) Having declared military assistance a priority in a time of emergency has equated the right to self-defense with an individual primary need for survival, giving it the status of a fundamental human right and putting armaments on the same level as basic humanitarian aid, such as food and shelter.
(3) The centrality of military and financial aid, though subjected to moralizing attitudes, still confirmed the realist assumption that inter-state aid can openly involve any kind of transfer between donor states and recipient states that is conducted on advantageous terms.
(4) The idea has emerged that in the context of warfare, *Aidization* is also extended to sanctions, coordinating the systematic use made of them in aid policies.

Anarchical Aid as a Key Component of War. The processes of Weaponization and Aidization carried out systematically and in the open have conceptually changed the very placement of inter-state aid among the main channels of international relations, beginning with *war* and *trade*. In particular, the Interventionist Aid did not fit into the previous categories of aid as the preferred and sustainable alternative to diverting any inevitable state power-political competition onto non-military terrain.

The Ukrainian war interrupted a decades-long continuum in which aid was considered as a viable alternative to military confrontation to the extent that, paraphrasing Carl Von Clausewitz's maxim about war being a continuation of politics by other means, the wide-ranging geopolitical competitions between donors in the transition and development scenarios had been defined using the term Aid Wars (Pellicciari, 2022a; Echevarria II, 2007; Allison, 2009).

After decades in which IAPPs had, in fact, been a continuation of war by other means, Interventionist Aid was officially framed as an organic, necessary, institutionalized part of an ongoing military conflict. It was an even more important turning point when linked to an apparently marginal historical fact. Drawing on the classic categories of realist thought, this fact can shed light on a particularly interesting and useful aspect that will be dealt with in the final pages of this article, i.e., those dedicated to the future of Interventionist Aid.

From a purely historical-political perspective, the harsh cross-criticism of the Weaponization of Aid and the Aidization of Weapons, levelled respectively by the West and Russia, could be dismissed as the effect of a frontal clash between two warring sides. This was also in all actuality a sign of a clear mutual refusal to recognize and accept the very idea of Russian Weaponization and Western Aidization, i.e., of new aid practices introduced by each side under the impetus and pressure of the war. This was done simply by dropping those new practices into the sides' pre-existing institutional narratives concerning aid policies.

Delegitimized because it lacked an international agreement regulating the minimum conditions of engagement, Interventionist Aid represents a decisive step backwards compared to the one that animated the old Aid Wars engaged in transition and development scenarios; the latter were fought with no holds barred but within a framework formalized by the multilateral dimension.

The rules of the game in the decades featuring Aid Wars were more descriptive than prescriptive and were broken more than once by the donors involved; nevertheless, they had the merit of identifying shared broad limits within which inter-state aid could be expressed. That held true whether the activity was humanitarian aid, development cooperation or in "other" fields such as military, financial, and technological assistance, etc.

By adopting a point of view featuring realist categories, it could be said that the rules regulating Aid Wars were an expression of an international order in the system of inter-state aid that was shattered by the Russian military invasion; moreover, the Interventionist Aid that followed called into question the minimum thresholds that had been agreed upon in the past.

Paraphrasing a pillar of Hedley Bull's realist thought, one could hypothesize that Interventionist Aid was born anarchic, insofar that it lacked a shared minimum regulatory principle the definition of which – according to the parties in the conflict – had not been previously delegated to the classic "neutral" multilateral institutions such as the UN (Bull, 1976). Such entities were excluded from being among the donor-protagonists in the Ukrainian war. Therefore, due to the unregulated nature of its main peculiarities, i.e., the Weaponization of Aid and the Aidization of Weapons, Interventionist Aid ideally marked the end of the non-military Aid Wars era; in so doing, it defined itself as a key, yet anarchical, component in an ongoing military conflict.

The Historical Dimension: The New "Interventionist Aid Phase"

The final consideration concerns the place of Interventionist Aid within the historical process of uninterrupted growth in the relevance of IAPPs over the last seven decades. This has been marked by the increase in public expenditure for the activation of IAPPs and the institutionalization of management structures both at the bilateral and multilateral levels.

While the political value of this aid has remained constant, the types of assistance rendered, and the characteristics of the actors have evolved in accordance with the general priorities declared by the interventions in each historical phase. The aforesaid evolutionary process took place over a timeframe that recently was simplified into three different historical phases: *Reconstruction Aid*, *Development Aid* and *Transition Aid*. This categorization effort was carried out based on the main keyword for aid in each period (Pellicciari, 2022a). Each of these phases circumscribed periods of varying duration during which the predominant types of aid did not completely replace one another but overlapped. Thus, new characteristics were added to those already entrenched.

Reconstruction Aid Phase. Predominant until the mid-1950s, this was a short and intense phase that largely coincided with the Marshall plan launched in the aftermath of the Second World War. Reconstruction was the keyword of aid, i.e., it was understood more as supportive lending than giving, and was instrumental to the declared primary objectives of US foreign policy (Hogan, 1987).

Development Aid Phase. This phase coincided with the long and steady period of Third World development cooperation policies of the 1960s and 1970s and served to assist the de-colonization processes of newly independent countries. In this period, aid policies became a prescriptive category, and were accompanied by the myth of Good Aid, with the overlapping idea of Foreign Aid featuring binomial terms: "cooperation + development" and "emergency + humanitarian" were consolidated.

Transition Aid Phase. This was the long phase that opened with the fall of the Berlin Wall, i.e., the end of the bipolar world order; from the 1990s onwards it was mainly defined, by post-war Transition Aid in the Western Balkans and post-Soviet Transition Aid in the former USSR. These were unprecedented scenarios of intervention in European territory, holding high geo-political value. These aid programs led to a change of pace in the growth of the use of aid in foreign policy, in the complication of the dynamics between donors and recipients, and in the different types of intervention carried out (Carbonnier, 2015).

Drawn up while the pandemic was still in progress and before war broke out in Ukraine, the above-mentioned periodization framework highlighted how Pandemic Aid could not be fully assimilated into the three phases that preceded it, though it retained accentuated political significance. Health-related emergency aid and Vaccine Diplomacy were treated as separate moments within the Transition Aid Phase, leaving open the question of whether Pandemic Aid was an isolated case or alternatively could signal the beginning of a new historical phase of inter-state aid. Two years onwards, formulating a hypothesis in this regard seems less arduous, in the light of the historical, seamless transition carried out from health emergency to war emergency and from Pandemic Aid to Interventionist Aid.

The common points highlighted between the two indicate a clear relationship between the scope of change in Interventionist Aid and the fact that it was preceded chronologically by Pandemic Aid. Seen from a historical perspective, the former fit into a pattern established by the latter, bringing to fruition and consolidating with technical and political peculiarities a new approach to IAPPs.

It thus continued along the same lines, i.e., influencing the course of events and the outcome of the crisis with unconventional aid disguised as classic Foreign Aid. Yet the Interventionist Aid model also significantly increased the determination, systematicity and spectrum of the aid mobilized.

Having characterized the two major global crises at the turn of the century, Pandemic Aid during Covid-19 and Interventionist Aid in the war that broke out in Ukraine, we can state that the implications stemming from them went far beyond their respective crisis contexts. Moreover, we are also able to assert that they became a model that could be applied by bilateral donors to other future contexts of geo-political interest.

The kind of consequential synergy that developed between Pandemic and Interventionist Aid suggests that the two were not merely passing blips on the screen of history, but rather the initiators of a new historical phase of IAPPs. The latter can ideally be defined as the Interventionist Aid Phase, highlighting the main feature of the IAPPs in the pandemic and the Ukrainian war; namely, the donors' determination to intervene by any means useful to affect the course of events in a crisis scenario.

The new phase therefore followed the Transition Aid Phase and yet, as in the previous phases, the imposition of the new Interventionist Aid model did not necessarily replace the previous models, but simply supplemented them. Furthermore, depending on the target scenario that the donors' action was intended to bring about, Interventionist Aid could co-exist with the others in a predominant or simply complementary position.

Postscript
The (Possible) Future of Interventionist Aid

It is generally not the task of historians to make predictions about the future of the subjects who's past they have studied whether in recent or remote history. It is a risky exercise that is seldom destined for success, and one worries about partaking at the urging of the infotainment industry; the latter does not hesitate to resort to the usual *escamotages* required to adapt a reading of yesterday to the needs of today in the name of gaining an audience.

It is common to question the historian as if he or she were an astrologer, forgetting that they are, if anything, more like astronomers, at ease with and more certain about the past than the future. There is, after all, a danger in implying a causal association between what *was*, what *is* or (even worse) what *will be*. If a particular object (or country) suddenly catches on fire, history helps to *understand* why it became flammable over time. Yet it certainly does not explain what sparked or who started the fire in the first place.

Despite this, and aware of the risks entailed by this endeavor, the exceptional nature of the elements that have emerged in this work prompts us to wager some basic projections about the possible medium-to long-term implications of the unprecedented case of Interventionist Aid that has characterized the Ukrainian scenario.

The following three brief reflections have been placed as an appendix to this work to signal the author's invitation to readers to separate their judgement on what has been written thus far from whether the forecasts expressed actually come true.

Interventionist Aid World Order

Marking a departure from the Transition Aid of previous decades, Interventionist Aid in Ukraine offered observers a privileged perspective within which to frame the main political dynamics of the international system at the time. While the conflict in question was circumscribed in the territorial sense, its impact on a global scale was the positioning of the main state actors precisely with respect to the aid given to Ukraine and the sanctions imposed on Russia (Sayapin, 2022, 768–70; Gioe and Styles, 2022).

After the initial, almost unanimous condemnation of the Russian invasion, the Ukrainian war also marked a global redefinition of power relations that reserved considerable surprises, such as the announcement in March 2023 of the agreement between Iran and Saudi Arabia mediated by China.

Considering the long lead times required for such initiatives, the high risk of those diplomatic talks falling apart for the slightest reason, and – specifically – that the agreement in questions was announced one year after the outbreak of war in Ukraine speaks of how the latter accelerated, rather than curbed, diplomatic processes that were already underway (Krickovic and Sakwa, 2022, 89–109; Sperling and Webber, 2017:19–46). Once again, in the first half of 2023 the significance of planned events such as Finland's entry into NATO and Syria's return to the Arab League spoke of the long-term changes underway in the international balance of power.

Fourteen months after the start of the war it seems that it is only a matter of time before these new equilibria consolidate into a new world order (Krickovic and Sakwa, 2022: 89–109; Gehring, 2022: 1489–1516; Haroche and Quencez, 2022: 73–86); Jankovic, 2022:107–35). As the latter encompasses among its constituent elements Interventionist Aid, said order could be characterized by:

- particularly pronounced impact of IAPPs on international relations;
- systematic recourse made to Interventionist Aid models, and not necessarily limited to emergency crisis scenarios;
- normalization of the tactical use of broad-based aid to achieve political objectives over primary, humanitarian ones;

- the predominance of the bilateral state dimension over the multilateral one;
- in the Western context: as a consequence of the Aidization of Weapons process, a contraction in classic Foreign Aid, in the non-governmental sector, and in the number of related service-providing consultants; furthermore, a strengthening of the private sector producing Interventionist Aid assets (mainly military and technological supplies, but also health services, etc);
- in the Eastern context: given the Weaponization of Aid, IAPPs remaining firmly in the public sector, and increased systematic use of primary goods and natural resources as offensive factors in hybrid wars on a bilateral basis; moreover, a further contraction of political and financial resources allocated at the multilateral level would occur.
- Despite such political and technical changes, institutional aid narratives will be slow to adapt, leading to the renewed formation of ideological polarization between a so-called Western Foreign Aid approach and an Eastern Foreign Gift one. That is, between Western donors who will place interventionist aid practices in the transitional categories of "Good Foreign Aid", and Eastern donors who, in contrast, will openly treat them as integral instruments of their own foreign policy.

Post-Democracy Aid

Aid policies would make it much more complicated for donor states to moralize and build popular consensus around their realism inspired foreign policy choices. Initially limited to bilateral state aid alone, over time the phenomenon would extend to non-governmental and multilateral aid as well.

Thus, there would be a crisis in the legitimacy of international aid due to its stronger politicization, the symptoms of which were initially manifested during the pandemic, but then re-emerged with the outbreak of the war in Ukraine. Their epicenter lay not so much in the concrete aid policies as in the inadequacy of the narratives that accompanied and the media system charged with disseminating them.

While the pandemic and the war in Ukraine introduced radical changes in aid policies, the public and institutional communication relating thereto remained anchored in the old development cooperation categories of the 1960s and 1970s; these have hardly changed since.

Faced with the difficulty of obtaining acceptance of foreign policy choices by a domestic public that is less ideologized and participatory, but more plagued by uncertainty and economic distress, donor states have chosen the easier option of relying on purely emotional and self-generated narratives relating to pandemic and war.

These narratives have largely experienced overexposure in the mainstream media and thus backfired, with negative effects for their messages; even when the latter are useful and necessary (as in the Covid-19 vaccination campaigns), at some point they have been experienced by the public as being so recurrent as to generate doubts and rejection. This crisis of trust in institutional narratives is common in the public opinions of an ever-growing number of donors states and has been exacerbated precisely during the pandemic crisis.

Moreover, unaddressed by the uninterrupted flow of emotional narratives, issues such as geopolitical and commercial interests related to vaccines or the huge disparity between the military and humanitarian aid deployed in Ukraine have been exempt from critical judgment, i.e., have therefore dangerously remained topics exclusively treated by social media.

Overburdened by the growing social tensions that any crisis with global impact inevitably brings with it, social media have developed alternative negative narratives built on the evident contradictions between the new interventionist aid approach and the rhetoric associated with the old established neutralist aid cultivated over decades of institutional communication.

It is for sociologists to analyze whether this crisis of aid narratives has constituted more cause than effect of the inability of traditional media to adapt to the times of the new communication platforms of the digital revolution.

What is certain is that the crisis of emotional aid narratives has been part of the broader context of a gradual erosion of legitimacy from which much of the world's leadership has long suffered, albeit to varying degrees.

Future systematic reliance on IAPPs in an interventionist sense would re-propose a widening of the gap between political and civil society, not so much because of the specific interventions involved *per se,* but because of the inability of classic international aid narratives to frame the new interventionism credibly.

Like health, welfare and labor policies, aid policies would enter the realm of political confrontation, removing them from the a-criticism that had been accorded to them in decades past, in the name of Neutralist Aid.

De-idealized in its purposes and rapidly becoming a politically divisive issue in both donor and recipient countries, Interventionist Aid will not be welcomed by a growing section of public opinion given that it will be perceived as having been imposed from above.

The orientation today that views inter-state aid through a negative lens, i.e., with both disenchanted and skeptical eyes, thus criticizing it as the result of post-democratic decision-making, will emerge strengthened and more widespread than ever (Crouch, 2020).

Whether real or perceived, *Post Democracy Aid* is slated to become a problem that will mainly concern Western donors, meaning those that have historically faced the problem of framing their state power politics in coherence with their own liberal-democratic founding values as well as classic Foreign Aid narratives.

In contrast, the problem of ex-post realignment on the universal values in their aid policies will involve so called Eastern Foreign Gift Donors to a lesser degree. The aforesaid have traditionally made open use of IAPPs for tactical purposes, declaring their political goals in advance, whether it was the supply on favorable terms of raw materials (or vaccines) for geopolitical purposes by Russia, or China's use of gift giving to achieve pure political obligation.

This could lead to a large-scale repetition of a paradoxical phenomenon already observed in recent crises. That is, substantial portions of Western public opinion, having become hypersensitive due to social media to the contradictions of their institutional domestic aid narratives compared to realist interventionist aid practices, may show respect, and sometimes sympathy, for the less rhetorical "straight talk" used by Eastern donors. Forgetting that the latter can state the political objectives of their aid in realist terms, precisely because they are less exposed to democratic electoral judgment of their choices. The culmination of the paradox will be in the political de-legitimization surrounding aid policies, being higher in those simply perceived as post-democratic rather than in those that are the certified result of a non-democratic process.

World War Aid

The final projection herein concerns the possible future consequences for the international system of a world order dominated by Interventionist Aid practices. In a nutshell, one can foresee a future in which the shift from (non-military) Aid Wars towards War Aid will be brought into the system and become a basic dynamic of international relations.

The mobilization of bilateral aid with overtly tactical and offensive strategies, has legitimized its use as a necessary key component of the war itself; permanently closing the Transition Aid Phase that, starting from the 1990s, had been able to hijack not only the competition but also the confrontation between donor states to the non-armed ground of the Aid Wars.

By reinforcing the link between IAPPs and the defense of state interests, it would open up the possibility of a future scenario in which Interventionist Aid could be the first choice applied by donors to all major scenarios of geopolitical interest.

The result would be a global-scale mushrooming of many real, long-lasting conflicts of alternating intensity, fought by recipient-partners on behalf of the respective donors; this due to the broad-spectrum aid provided by the latter. In such a scenario, much of the international system could progressively slide into a future stage of World War Aid, somewhat reminiscent of the Cold War in terms of the widespread level of circumscribed conflicts fought over various crises. And with the big players playing remotely.

However, the hypothetical scenario outlined above would present considerably complicated structural and political elements compared to the past. On the one hand, we would have the impact of the enormous increase and development of technological, military, and financial assets that could potentially be used as aid. Moreover, the growth in demand for – and therefore the importance of – raw materials and natural resources on a global level would be a factor. Indeed, the latter are destined to grow in the future rather than decline.

On the other hand, compared to the simplified rigidity of the past US–USSR balance of power, Interventionist Aid would feature a larger number of various-sized actors among the protagonists who have, in recent decades, sought (and often managed) to increase their international status through prominence in inter-state aid, either as donors or strategic recipients. For example, while the dissolution of just two countries, the USSR and the SFY Yugoslavia, gave birth to 22 new sovereign states each with its own foreign policy, other cases such as that of the Republic of San Marino demonstrated that, in a geopolitical competition played out on the interventionism of vaccines sent as aid, even a few thousand doses distributed over a 61-square meter micro-state had sufficient global relevance to earn headlines in the *Washington Post* (Pellicciari, 2022a, 92–96).

Politically, the main problem will remain the lack of shared minimum rules of engagement of major Interventionist Aid practices such as the Weaponization of Aid and the Aidization of Weapons, exacerbated by the shift in geopolitical axes from Central Europe westward to the United States and eastward to Asia and a Chinese-driven *Greater Eurasia* (Krickovic and Pellicciari, 2021: 86–99).

Unlike past Aid Wars, (Interventionist) War Aid would sanction the total incompatibility between a Western front that frames its intervention as defense of the liberal rules-based order, and an Eastern one that contextualizes its intervention as the explicit foreign policy goal of reducing Anglo-Saxon international predominance in favor of a new multipolar order (Geis and Schröder, 2023: 1–13; Freedman, 2022; Way, 2022: 5–17; Lukyanov, 2023: 5–10, Karaganov, 2022: 50–67; Sakwa, 2017).

This hypothetical scenario of World War Aid spread over multiple low-intensity conflicts fought through interventionist aid and in the absence of clearly defined rules but within a world order being defined by these deployments, simultaneously represents a somber vision, but one that is also consoling.

It is gloomy in that it suggests the possibility of a regression in international relations to a context presenting tolerated and accepted widespread nineteenth–century-style conflicts and an emptying of the meaning of human, political, and social terms and rights that had been taken for granted, had been considered immovable.

On the other hand, just as when after fearing the worst one rejoices in the "less bad", so the vision of a World War fought through aid banishes the prospect of a Third World War fought with nuclear weapons.

The former prospect would be no less harsh, but at least the world would be less at risk of facing the end of everything.

Bibliography

Allison, R. (2013) *Russia, the West, and Military Intervention*, Oxford: Oxford University Press.

Annen, K.M. and Moers, L. (2012) "Donor Competition for Aid Impact, and Aid Fragmentation", *IMF Working Papers* 12/204.

Bakalova, E., Spanger, H. and Neumann, J. M. (2013) *Development Cooperation or Competition? Russia as a re-emerging donor* PRIF Report No. 123. Frankfurt/M.

Bélanger, M.E. (2022) "What prospect is there of Ukraine joining the EU?" *LSE European Politics and Policy (EUROPP) blog*

Bosse, G. (2022) "Values, rights, and changing interests: The EU's response to the war against Ukraine and the responsibility to protect Europeans", *Contemporary Security Policy* 43(3), 531–46

Brezhneva, A.; Ukhova, D. (2013) *Russia as a Humanitarian Aid Donor*, Oxfam International.

Bull, H. (2012) *The Anarchical Society. A Study of Order in World Politics*, Fourth Edition, New York: Columbia University Press.

Burg, S.L.; Shoup, P. (1999) *The War in Bosnia-Herzegovina: Ethnic Conflict and International Intervention*, New York: Routledge

Carbonnier, Gilles. 2015. *Humanitarian Economics: War, Disaster and the Global Aid Market*, Oxford: Oxford University Press.

Carmichael, C. (2015) *A Concise History of Bosnia*, Cambridge: Cambridge University Press.

Carr, E.H. (1939) *The Twenty Years' Crisis, 1919–1939: An Introduction to the Study of International Relations*, Edinburgh: R&R Clark.

Cavandoli, S. and Wilson, G. (2022) "Distorting fundamental norms of international law to resurrect the Soviet Union: The international law context of Russia's invasion of Ukraine", *Netherlands International Law Review* 69, 383–410.

Chohan, U.W. (2021) Coronavirus & Vaccine Nationalism, *CASS Working Papers on Economics & National Affairs*

Bibliography

Craven, M.C. (1995) "The European Community Arbitration Commission on Yugoslavia", *British Yearbook of International Law* 66(1), 333–413.

Crawford, N.C. (2015) *The Dangerous Leap: Preventive War. Lessons from Iraq*, Abingdon: Routledge.

Crawford, P. and Bryce, P. (2003) "Project monitoring and evaluation: A method for enhancing the efficiency and effectiveness of aid project implementation", *International Journal of Project Management* 21(5), 363–73.

Crouch, C. (2020) *Post-Democracy After the Crises*, Cambridge: Polity Press

D'Anieri, P. (2003) "Leonid Kuchma and the personalisation of the Ukrainian presidency", *Problems of Post-Communism* 50(5), 58–65.

Dahlman, C. and Toal G. (2005) *Bosnia Remade: Ethnic Cleansing and its Reversal*, Oxford: Oxford University Press.

Depledge, D. (2021) "NATO and the Arctic: the need for a new approach", *The RUSI Journal* 165(5–6), 80–90.

De Ploeg, C. K. (2017) *Ukraine in the Crossfire*, Atlanta: Clarity Press, Inc.

Dhawan, M., Choudhary, O.P. and Saied, A.A. (2022) "Russo-Ukrainian war amid the COVID-19 pandemic: Global impact and containment strategy", *International Journal of Surgery* 102, 106675.

Dräger, L., Gründler K. and Potrafke, N. (2022) *Political Shocks and Inflation Expectations: Evidence from the 2022 Russian Invasion of Ukraine*, CESifo Working Paper, 9649, Munich: CESifo

Dreyer, I. and Popescu, N. (2014) "Do Sanctions Against Russia Work?" *European Union Institute for Security Studies* (EUISS)

Echevarria II, A.J. (2007) *Clausewitz and Contemporary War*, Oxford: Oxford University Press.

Estrada, M.A.R. and Koutronas, E. (2022) "The impact of the Russian Aggression against Ukraine on the Russia-EU Trade", *Journal of Policy Modelling* 44(3), 599–616.

Fagan, A. (2006) "Civil society in Bosnia ten years after Dayton", *International Peacekeeping* 12(3), 406–19.

Fidler, D.P. (2020) "Vaccine nationalism's politics", *Science* 369(6505), 749.

Freedman, L. (2022) "Why war fails: Russia's invasion of Ukraine and the limits of military power", *Foreign Affairs* 101(10).

Furia, A. (2015) *The Foreign Aid Regime: Gift-Giving, States and Global Dis/Order*, New York: Palgrave MacMillan

Galus, A. (2020) "What is media assistance and (why) does it matter? The case of Polish foreign aid to the media in Belarus and Ukraine", *Central European Journal of Communication* 13(27), 390–408.

Geis, A. and Schröder, U. (2023) "Global consequences of the war in Ukraine: the last straw for (liberal) interventionism?", *Zeitschrift für Friedens-und Konfliktforschung*, 1–13.

Gehring, K. (2022) "Can external threats foster a European Union identity? Evidence from Russia's invasion of Ukraine", *The Economic Journal* 132(644), 1489–516.

Gilbert, A.C. (2016) "From humanitarianism to humanitarianization: Intimacy, estrangement, and international aid in postwar Bosnia and Herzegovina", *American Ethnologist* 43(4), 717–29.

Gioe, D.V., Styles, W. (2022) "Vladimir Putin's Russian world turned upside down", *Armed Forces & Society* Available at: https://doi.org/10.1177/0095327X221121778

Glaurdić, J. (2011) *The Hour of Europe: Western Powers and the Breakup of Yugoslavia,* New Haven: Yale University Press.

Gould-Davies, N. (2020) "Russia, the West and sanctions", *Survival* 62(1), 7–28.

Götz, L., Glauben, T., and Brümmer, B. (2013) "Wheat export restrictions and domestic market effects in Russia and Ukraine during the food crisis", *Food Policy* 38, 214–26.

Gray, Patty A. (2015) "Russia as a recruited development donor", *The European Journal of Development Research* 27(2), 273–88.

Grossi, Giuseppe and Vakulenko, Veronika (2022) "New development: Accounting for human-made disasters – comparative analysis of the support to Ukraine in times of war", *Public Money & Management* 42(6), 467–71.

Hall, N. and Lang, H. (2023) "The Weaponisation of Humanitarian Aid", *Foreign Affairs*. Available at: www.foreignaffairs.com/world/weaponization-humanitarian-aid

Hall, I. (2006) *The International Thought of Martin Wight*, London: Palgrave Macmillan.

Hansen, L. (2006) *Security as Practice: Discourse Analysis and the Bosnian War*, London: Routledge.

Haroche, P.; Quencez M. (2022) "NATO facing China: Responses and adaptations", *Survival* 64(3), 73–86.

Hashimova, U. (2022) *Ukraine: The View from Central Asia*, Available at: https://thediplomat.com/2022/03/ukraine-the-viewfrom-central-asia/

Hill, M.A. (2011) *Democracy Promotion and Conflict-Based Reconstruction: The United States & Democratic Consolidation in Bosnia, Afghanistan & Iraq*, London: Routledge.

Hogan, Michael J. 1987. *The Marshall Plan. America, Britain, and the Reconstruction of Western Europe 1947–1952*, Cambridge: Cambridge University Press.

Huntington, S.P. (1971) "Foreign aid, for what and for whom", *Foreign Policy* (1) 161–89.

Janković, S. (2022) "Odjeci Ukrainskog rata na Bliskom Istoku", *National Interest*, XVII (43) 107–35.

Jović, D. (2009) *Yugoslavia: A State That Withered Away*, West Lafayette: Purdue University Press.

Kalyanpur, N. (2020) *Liberalism Outsourced: Why Oligarchs and Autocrats Fight in Foreign Courts*, Washington D.C.: Georgetown University.

Karaganov, S.A. (2022) "From Constructive Destruction to Gathering", *Russia in Global Affairs* 20(1), 50–67.
Kennan, G. (1947) "The sources of Soviet conduct", *Foreign Affairs* 25(4), 566–82.
Kissinger, H. (2014) *World Order*, London: Penguin.
Kobayashi, Y., Heinrich, T. and Bryant, K.A. (2021) "Public support for development aid during the COVID-19 pandemic", World Development 138.
Korhonen, I, Simola, H. and Solanko, L. (2018) Sanctions, counter-sanctions and Russia: Effects on economy, trade and finance, *Bank of Finland Institute for Emerging Economies Policy Brief*, 4.
Krickovic, A. and Pellicciari, I. (2021) "From Greater Europe to Greater Eurasia. Status concerns and the evolution of Russia's approach to alignment and regional integration", *Journal of Eurasian Studies* 12(1), 86–99. doi: https://doi.org/10.1177%2F1879366521998808
Krickovic, A. and Sakwa, R. (2022) "War in Ukraine: The Clash of Norms and Ontologies", *Journal of Military and Strategic Studies* 22(2), 89–109.
Kubicek, P. (2005) "The European Union and democratisation in Ukraine", *Communist and Post-communist Studies* 38(2), 269–92.
Kubicek, P. (2008) *The History of Ukraine*, Westport CT: Greenwood Press.
Kudelia, S. (2014) "The Maidan and beyond: The house that Yanukovych built", *Journal of Democracy* 25(3), 19–34.
Larionova, M., Rakhmangulov, M. and Berenson, M.P. (2016) "Russia: A Re-emerging Donor", *The BRICS in International Development*, London: Palgrave Macmillan, 63–92.
Levy, J.S. (2011) "Preventive war: Concept and propositions", *International Interactions* 37(1), 87–96.
Lukyanov, F.A. (2023) "Between two special operations", *Russia in Global Affairs* 21(2), 5–10.
Malchrzak, W., et al. (2022) "COVID-19 Vaccination and Ukrainian refugees in Poland during Russian-Ukrainian War. A narrative review", *Vaccines* 10(6), 955.
Masters, J. (2022) "Ukraine: Conflict at the crossroads of Europe and Russia", *Council on Foreign Relations* 1.
Mbah, R.E., and Wasum, D.F. (2022) "Russian-Ukraine 2022 War: A review of the economic impact of Russian-Ukraine crisis on the USA, UK, Canada, and Europe", *Advances in Social Sciences Research Journal* 9(3), 144–53.
Mearsheimer, J.J. (2014) "Why the Ukraine crisis is the West's fault: the liberal delusions that provoked Putin", *Foreign Affairs* 93(5), 77–89.
Mills, C. (2022) *Military Assistance to Ukraine since the Russian Invasion*, London: Research Briefing, House of Commons Library, 9477.

Milner, H.V. (2006) "Why multilateralism? Foreign aid and domestic principal-agent problems" in Hawkins, D.G. et al. (eds) *Delegation and Agency in International Organizations*. New York: Cambridge University Press, 107–39.

Minakov, M., Kasianov, G., and Rojansky M. (eds) (2021) *From "The Ukraine" to Ukraine, A Contemporary History, 1991–2021*, Stuttgart: Ibidem Verlag.

Morgenthau, H. (1962) "A Political Theory of Foreign Aid", *American Political Science Review* 56(2), 301–09.

Morgenthau, H. (1978) *Politics Among Nations: The Struggle for Power and Peace, 6 Principles of Political Realism*, 5th Edition, New York: Alfred A. Knopf.

O'Ballance, E. (1995) *Civil War in Bosnia 1992–94*, London: Palgrave Macmillan.

Odey, S.A.; Samuel A.B. (2022) "Ukrainian Foreign Policy toward Russia between 1991 and 2004: The Start of the Conflict", *Journal of Liberty and International Affairs* 8, 346.

Olsson, C. (2015) "Interventionism as Practice: On 'Ordinary Transgressions' and their Routinization". *Journal of Intervention and Statebuilding* 9(4), 425–41.

O'Meara, K. (2022) "Understanding the illegality of Russia's invasion of Ukraine". Available at: https://studycorgi.com/understanding-the-illegality-of-russias-invasion-of-ukraine-article-analysis/

Özler, Ş. (2020) "The United Nations at seventy-five: Passing the COVID test?", *Ethics & International Affairs* 34(4), 445–56.

Pellicciari, I. (2017) "Feeding the Trojan Horse: International Aid Policies in support to NGOs (1990–2015)" in Marchetti, R. (ed.) *Partnership in International Policy Making*, New York: Palgrave MacMillan, 293–310.

Pellicciari, I. (2021) "The Poor Donor and the Rich Recipient. Foreign Aid and Donor's Competition in the COVID-19 Era". In *International Organizations and States Response to COVID-19*, Belgrade: Institute of International Politics and Economics, 267–77.

Pellicciari, I. (2022a) *Re-framing Foreign Aid History and Politics: From the Fall of the Berlin Wall to the COVID-19 Outbreak*, Abingdon: Routledge.

Pellicciari, I. (2022b) "Aid in War or Aid to War, Foreign Aid in the 2022 War in Ukraine", *Review of International Affairs*, vol. LXXIII, No. 1186, 61–78.

Pickering, P.M. (2014) "Explaining the Varying Impact of International Aid for Local Democratic Governance in Bosnia-Herzegovina", *Problems of Post-Communism* 59(1), 31–43.

Pishchikova, K. (2010) *Promoting Democracy in Post-communist Ukraine: The Contradictory Outcomes of US Aid to Women's NGOs*, Boulder CO: Lynne Rienner Publishers.

Radeljić, B. (2012) *Europe and the Collapse of Yugoslavia: The Role of Non-State Actors and European Diplomacy*, London: Palgrave Macmillan
Ramboll (2009) "Evaluation of the EU Decentralised Agencies in 2009: Agency level findings", Evaluation for the European Commission. Available at: www.europarl.europa.eu/meetdocs/2009_2014/documents/libe/dv/evaluation_eu_agencies_vol_iii_/evaluation_eu_agencies_vol_iii_en.pdf
Republic of Poland (2022) High-level International Donors' Conference for Ukraine, Available at: www.gov.pl/web/canada-en/high-level-international-donors-conferencefor-ukraine---thursday-5-may-2022-in-warsaw
Ringsmose, J. and Rynning, S. (2021) "NATO's next strategic concept: Prioritise or perish", *Survival* 63(5), 147–68.
Roberts, G. (2022) "Now or Never: The immediate origins of Putin's preventative war on Ukraine", *Journal of Military and Strategic Studies* 22(2), 3–27.
Rogel, C. (1998) *The Breakup of Yugoslavia and the War in Bosnia*, Westport CT: Greenwood Publishing Group.
Rogel, C. (2004) *The Breakup of Yugoslavia and its Aftermath*, Westport CT: Greenwood Publishing Group.
Rutland, P. (2014) "The impact of sanctions on Russia", *Russian Analytical Digest* 157(1), 1–8.
Sakwa R. (2017) *Russia Against the Rest: The Post-Cold War Crisis of World Order*, Cambridge: Cambridge University Press, 2017.
Sapir, A. (2022) "Ukraine and the EU: Enlargement at a new crossroads", *Intereconomics* 57(4), 213–17.
Sayapin, S. (2022) "Russia's invasion of Ukraine: a test for international law", *Nature Human Behaviour* 6(6), 768–70.
Schuette, L.A. (2021) "Why NATO survived Trump: the neglected role of Secretary General Stoltenberg", *International Affairs* 97(6), 1863–81.
Sperling, J. and Webber, M. (2017) "NATO and the Ukraine crisis: Collective securitization", *European Journal of International Security* 2(1), 19–46.
Strazzari, F. (2022) *Frontiera Ucraina. Guerra, geopolitiche e ordine internazionale*, Bologna: Il Mulino.
Subtelny, O. (2009) *Ukraine: A History Fourth Edition*, Toronto: University of Toronto Press.
Szőke, J. and Kolos K. (2023) "Military Assistance to Ukraine and Its Significance in the Russo-Ukrainian War", *Social Sciences* 12(5), 294.
Trebesch, C., Antezza, A., Bushnell, K., Frank, A., Frank, P., Franz, L., Kharitonov, I., Kumar,B., Rebinskaya, E., and Schramm, S. (2023) "The Ukraine Support Tracker: Which countries help Ukraine and

how?" *Kiel Working Paper* 2218. Kiel: Kiel Institute for the World Economy.
Tsygankov, A. (2016) *Russia's Foreign Policy: Change and Continuity in National Identity*, New York: Rowman & Littlefield.
Waltz, K. (1979) *Theory of International Politics*, Reading: Addison-Wesley Publishing.
Way, L.A. (2022) "The Rebirth of the Liberal World Order?", *Journal of Democracy* 33(2), 5–17.
Wedel, J.R. (2001) *Collision and Collusion: The Strange Case of Western Aid to Eastern Europe*. New York: Palgrave MacMillan.
Wight, M. (1978) *Power Politics*, London: Continuum International Publishing Group, Royal Institute of International Affairs.
Woehrel, S. (2014) Ukraine: current issues and US policy, Library of Congress Washington DC Congressional Research Service.
Wolczuk, K. (2004) "Integration without Europeanisation: Ukraine and its policy towards the European Union", *European University Institute, EUI Working Papers*, RSCAS 2004/15 (2004), 1–22.
Wolff, A.T. (2015) "The future of NATO enlargement after the Ukraine crisis", *International Affairs* 91(5), 1103–21
Wolff, S.; Ladi, S. (2020) "European Union responses to the Covid-19 pandemic: Adaptability in times of permanent emergency", *Journal of European Integration* 42(8), 1025–40.
Yushkov, A., Oding, N. and Savulkin, L. (2017) "The trajectories of donor regions in Russia", *Voprosy Economiki* 9, 63–82.

Index

Note: Page numbers in **bold** refers to Tables.

aid during wartime: anarchical aid as key component of war, 9, 125–128; inter-state aid in Ukraine war as turning point in, 92; lack of conditions for military aid and, 86–87; military aid in post-WWII peacetime, 92; traditional aid, 85–86; visibility/secrecy of military bilateral cooperation pre-Ukraine, 92–93; World War Aid as potential future impact of Interventionist Aid, 10–11, 136–138. *See also* Interventionist Aid; military aid and training; Western bilateral aid/donors in Ukraine 2022

aid peculiarities. *See* Interventionist Aid; peculiarities

Aid to Ukraine (1991–2021), 5, 22–23; change in 2014 due to Crimea and Yanukovich removal, 6, 24, 37; competition between Russian and Western donors and, 6, 24–25, 37–38; as historical early symptom of Ukraine war, 5, 21; historical-political relevance of, 4–5, 9–10, 111–112; peculiarities in, 5–8, 11–12, 21, 25, **71**; phases of, 5–6, 25; as turning point in inter-state aid, 1–3, 21, 92; Western economic cooperation emphasis *vs.* liberal-democratic development, 6, 25–27, 30, 35–36. *See also Aid without Reforms Phase* (1991–2004); *Atlanticist Strategy Phase* (2014–2022); Interventionist Aid; Interventionist Aid *vs.* Pandemic Aid; *Pro-European Ambition Phase* (2005–2010); Ukraine 2022 *vs.* Bosnia and Herzegovina 1992; Ukraine war (2022); *War of Aid Phase* (2010–2014); Western bilateral aid/donors in Ukraine 2022

Aid without Reforms Phase (1991–2004), 5–6, 25–31; EU aid agreements during *vs.* current agreements, 27–28; EU aid programs during, 28–29; *Gore-Kuchma Commission* and, 30; Russian "neighborhood policy" and, 31; Russian aid as natural/financial resources during, 26–27, 30; Russian Commonwealth of Independent States (CIS) Charter and, 31; TACIS program and, 28–29, 33; USAID during 1991 to 1995, 29; USAID during 2001 to 2004, 29–30

aid, comparative, 4–5
aid, use of term post-2022: infotainment and, 16–17, 94
Aidization of sanctions, 7–8, 67, 103–108
Aidization of weapons, 7, 66, 92; defined, 9, 68. *See also* Western Aidization of weapons
Anarchical aid, as key component of war, 9, 125–128
anti-corruption reform: EU agenda of during 2005–2010, 33; EU agenda of during 2014–2022, 38–39, 42–43; National Reunification reforms and, 40–42; Western donor agenda of during 2010–2014, 35–37
anti-oligarch law, 41
Association Agreement (AA, EU-Ukraine), 32, 38–39, 42; suspension of by Brussels, 37
Atlanticist Strategy Phase (2014–2022), 6, 25, 37; Association Agreement (AA, EU-Ukraine) and, 38–39, 42; EBRD, IMF and WB priorities during, 39; Maidan Revolution and, 26, 38; military cooperation programs post-Crimea annexation and, 43–44; National Reunification reforms during, 40–41; pro-Western/anti-Russian stance in, 38; Russian aid post-Crimea and, 44; Ukraine's future integration into EU/NATO and, 26, 42–43; Western aid conditionality and regulatory framework conditions, 38–40; Western aid continuation despite lack of reform, 41–43; Zelensky presidency reforms and policies and, 40–41
autonomy of Ukrainian government, 80–81

Biden, President Joe, 79
Big Pharma, 2

BiH war, comparative aid with Ukraine. *See* Ukraine 2022 *vs.* Bosnia and Herzegovina 1992
black market for arms, military supplies to Kyiv and, 87
Bull, Hedley, 128
Bush Administration, 54

casualties, civilian: estimations of Ukraine War *vs.* Covid-19, 1; in Ukraine 2022 *vs.* BiH 1992, 64
China: mediation by, 132; military aid to Russia from, 118
classic foreign aid: "Good Aid" myth, 11, 129; *vs.* International Aid Public Policies (IAPPs), 19–20; Interventionist and Pandemic Aid and, 115; interventionist creation of new principles/justifications for military aid and, 95–96, 125; military aid in post-WWII peacetime, 92; military aid to Ukraine and, 94–95; shift to War Aid as possible future impact of Interventionist Aid, 136–138. *See also* aid during wartime
Clinton, Bill, 79
Commonwealth of Independent States (CIS) Charter, 31
competition: between donor states, 6, 12, 24–25, 37–38; donor-recipient, 4; of donors over reconstruction of Ukraine post-conflict, 99–101; in Vaccine Diplomacy, 117, 119–120
corruption: *Corruption Perception Index*, 36; military aid to Kyiv and, 87–88. *See also* anti-corruption reform
Covid-19, 5; unpreparedness of UN for, 113–114; vaccine diplomacy of West *vs.* aid at outbreak of war, 1–3, 73–74; vaccine diplomacy of West *vs.* Russia, 1–3, 20. *See also* Interventionist Aid *vs.*

Pandemic Aid; Pandemic Aid; Vaccine Diplomacy
Crimea annexation, 38, 43–44; as break point in pro-Western *vs.* pro-Russian alliances, 6, 38

Dayton Peace Accords, 62, 99, 105
Declaration of Aid Effectiveness (2007), 34
De Hoop Scheffer, Jaap, 33
denuclearization, 27
Donbas area of Ukraine, 24, 38, 43–44
Donor-Driven Processes, shift in, 79–81
Donor-Recipient Partnership: *vs.* Recipient-Driven Aid, **121**, 123–124
Donor-Recipient peculiarities: in Ukraine *vs.* BiH War, 64–65
Draghi, Mario, 79, 101, 114

energy resources, Russian aid to Ukraine and: in 1991–2004 phase, 26–27, 30; in 2014–2022 phase, 44; as Russian hybrid weapon, 7, 66
EU-Ukraine Action Plan (2005), 28, 32
European Neighborhood Policy (ENP), 32
European Union (EU): aid peculiarities and, 114; Association Agreement (AA, EU-Ukraine) and, 32, 37–39, 42; EU membership for Ukraine proposals, 26, 42–43, 66, 98–99, 101–103; *EU-Ukraine Action Plan* (2005), 28–29, 32; *European Neighborhood Policy* (ENP), 32; Interventionist Aid and, 119; Macro-Financial Assistance (MFA) to Ukraine, 42, 83, 87; military aid to Ukraine, 84–85; pandemic aid to Ukraine, 85; PCA agreement and, 28–29, 32; political disinterest in Ukraine phase (1991–2004), 6, 27–29; political disinterest in Ukraine phase (2005–2010), 32–33; renouncing of aid in 2013, 37; sanctions and, 104, 115; TACIS program of, 28–29, 33; visit of Zelensky to, 81–82. *See also* Pro-European Ambition Phase (2005–2010); Western *Aidization of weapons*

food, as hybrid weapon, 91–92
foreign policy, aid as instrument of for donor states, 4, 12, 19, 34, 73, 95; future of under new world order of Interventionist Aid, 9–11, 112, 131–133; historical-political relevance of Ukraine war aid and, 4–5, 9–10, 111–112; replacement of *neutrality* by *interventionism* and, 76–77; Russian *Weaponization of Aid* and, 90; in Ukraine 2022 *vs.* BiH War in 1992, 67, 73–75; *Vaccine Diplomacy* and, 19–20
freedom of speech, 41

German aid, 80–81
"Good Aid" myth, 11, 129
Gore-Kuchma Commission, 30
guerilla warfare in Eastern Ukraine, 24, 38, 44

Hobbes, Thomas, 19
humanitarian aid: *vs.* geo-political concerns in Ukraine 2022 *vs.* BiH war, 1–3, 67–69, 73–77, 85, 93–94; Interventionist Aid overshadowing of, 11–12, 67–69, 73–77, 84, 92, 95; legitimizing of priority status of military aid over, 86–87, 92–96; non-necessity of in Ukraine since late 1990s, 74; relegation of, 7, 65–68, 83; relegation of to Western reconstruction bidding, 96–97; Vaccine Diplomacy and,

1–3; wheat as center of since end of WWII, 91
hybrid weapon, classic aid goods as, 7, 9, 66, 68, 90–91, 125

Index of Economic Freedom, 36
infotainment: use of word *aid* and, 16–17, 94
International Aid Public Policies (IAPPs): *aidization of weapons*, 9; *vs.* classic foreign aid, 8, 19–20; as conceptual dimension of *Interventionist Aid*, 8–9; Donor-Recipient Partnership *vs.* Recipient-Driven Aid in evolution of, **121**, 123–124; as driver in international relations, 119, 122; Interventionist Aid as radical turning point in, 116; Interventionist and Pandemic Aid commonalities and, 119–120; lack of shared agreement of new modalities of in Interventionist *vs.* Pandemic Aid, 117; political evolution of, **121**, 121–124; realist approach of in study, 8, 11–12, 19–22, **121**, 122, 124–128; Success-Oriented Aid in evolution of, 8, **121**, 122–124; Ukrainian Interventionist Aid model in evolution of, 3–5, **121**, 121–122; *weaponization of aid* and, 9. See also Western bilateral aid/donors in Ukraine 2022
international relations: "preventive intervention" as dangerous concept for future, 95; aid as instrument of, 19, 92; future of under new world order of Interventionist Aid, 9–11, 112, 131–133; historical-political relevance of Ukraine war aid and, 4–5, 9–10, 111–112; IAPPs as driver in, 119, 122; in Interventionist Aid *vs.* Pandemic Aid, 111–112; interventionist military aid's creation of new principles/justifications in, 95–96; strong impact of aid on, 19; Ukraine War as redefining, 15, 112, 133; Vaccine Diplomacy and, 19–20
Interventionist Aid: "preventive intervention" as dangerous concept for future, 95; *aidization of weapons* as new conceptual practice of, 9, **121**, 125–128; anarchical aid as key component of war (conceptual dimension), 9, 125–128; competition between donor states under *vs.* "Good" Foreign Aid modalities, 12; Donor-Recipient Partnership *vs.* Recipient-Driven Aid, **121**, 123–124; as effect of war in Ukraine, 3–5, 12, 76, 86, 126; eight peculiarities of, 5–8, 11–12, 21, 70–108, **71**, 92, 116, 121, 124, 128; EU and, 119; future potential impacts of, 9–11, 131–136; geo-political *vs.* humanitarian reordering as potential future impact of, 1–3, 9–11, 73, 122, 132; historical dimension as "Interventionist Aid Phase," **121**, 128–130; International Aid Public Policies (IAPPs) as conceptual dimension of, 8–9; lack of shared agreement of new modalities of, 117, 127; NATO and, 119; *vs.* Neutralist Aid, 67–69, 75–77; new practices of political dimensions of, 8; new world order based on as potential future impact, 9–11, 131–133; as overcoming historical Transition Aid, 9, 129–130, 132, 136; overshadowing of humanitarian aid in, 11–12, 67–69, 73–77, 84, 92, 95; political evolution of IAPPs and, **121**, 121–124; Post-democracy Aid as

potential future impact of, 10, 133–136; realist approach of in study of Interventionist *vs.* Pandemic Aid, 20–22, 124; realist theoretical approach in study of IAPPs, 8, 11–12, 19–22, **121**, 122, 124–128; Recipient-Driven Aid and, 8; shift to War Aid as potential future impact of, 136–138; Success-Oriented Aid in evolution of IAPPs and, 8, **121**, 122–124; technical-political peculiarities in, 68, 96, 99, 121, 124; of Ukraine 2022 *vs.* Neutralist Aid of BiH War 1992, 21, 67–69; Ukrainian government as equal partner and sole recipient of Western bilateral aid as, 7–8, 65, **71**, 72, 77–82, 105–106, 124; *weaponization of aid* as new conceptual practice of, 9, 84, **121**, 125–128; Western *Aidization of weapons* as constituent element of, 12, 68–69, 117, 125; World War Aid as potential future impact of, 10–11, 136–138. *See also* Western bilateral aid/donors in Ukraine 2022

Interventionist Aid *vs.* Pandemic Aid, 3–5, 85, **118**; aid peculiarities and, 110, 114, 116, **118**, 129; bilateral donor prominence over NGOs/international orgs and, 112–115; centrality of aid (IAPPs) in *vs.* past crises, 111, 120; compared with Ukrainian Aid *vs.* BiH war aid, 120; as differing crisis and outcomes, 15; as dual crisis scenario, 14; frequency of word *aid* and, 15–16; future scenarios predictions for, 22; IAPPs' impact on, 119–120; international relations impact and, 111–112; Interventionist Aid as radical turning point in IAPPs, 116; lack of shared agreement of new modalities, 117–118; non-governmental aid as unreliable perspective for study on, 17–18; Pandemic Aid as traditional aid, 116–117; political aspects of Pandemic Aid and, 19–20, 111–112; realist theoretical approach of IAPP concept and, 19–22; unconventionality of aid policies/interventions, 115; Vaccine Diplomacy and, 19–20, 73–74, 115, 117; Western reactions and, 1–3. *See also* Pandemic Aid

Iran: military aid to from Russia and, 118; new partnerships of, 132

Italy, 82, 101; Sputnik-V vaccine in, 2; Vaccine Diplomacy and, 2, 117

judiciary reform: EU agenda of during 2014–2022, 38–39, 43; EU donor agenda during 2005–2010, 33; National Reunification reforms and, 40–41; Western donor agenda of during 2010–2014, 35–37

Jushenko, Viktor, 31; US political support of in 2003, 33–34

Karzai, Hamid, 82

Kravchuk, President Leonid, 26. *See also Aid without Reforms Phase* (1991–2004)

Kuchma, President Leonid, 26, 35; *Gore-Kuchma Commission* and, 30. *See also Aid without Reforms Phase* (1991–2004)

Kuleba, Dmytro, 78, 80–81, 101

Kyiv, foreign leaders' journeys to, 79. *See also* Aid to Ukraine (1991–2021); pro-Russian Kyiv governments; pro-Western Kyiv governments; Ukraine war (2022); Ukrainian government

Lavrov, Sergey, 90
Leopard 2 tanks, 80

Machiavelli, Niccolò, 19
Macro-Financial Assistance (MFA), 42, 83, 87
Macron, Emmanuel, 79
Maidan Revolution, 26, 37–38, 77
Marshall Plan, 128
media: Ukrainian appeals for weapons in, 80–81; Western coverage of Ukraine War outbreak and, 79–81; Western in Ukraine 2022 *vs.* BiH 1992, 58–61
Meloni, Giorgia, 101
military aid and training, 83–85, 92; corruption and embezzlement concerns and, 87–88; danger of legitimizing, 95; interventionist creation of new justifications for, 95–96, 125; lack of conditions for, 86–87; legitimizing of priority status of over humanitarian aid, 86–87, 92, 94–96; military cooperation programs, 43–44; peculiarity of predominance of, 94; in post-WWII peacetime, 92; potential future implications of, 94; refusal to give in BiH war, 93; to Russia from China, India, Iran, 118; before Ukraine War, 92–93; Western *Aidization of weapons* and, 92–96. See also Western *Aidization of weapons*
Milošević, Slobodan, 105, 108
multilateral cooperation, Russian divorce from, 90–91

Naletilić, Mladen ("Tuta"), 63
National Anticorruption Strategy (2011–2015), 36
National Reunification reforms, 40–42
NATO, 26; aid peculiarities and, 114; Finland's entry to, 132; Interventionist Aid and, 119; during pandemic, 74; Ukraine's future integration into, 26, 42–43
natural resources, Russian aid to Ukraine and, 24, 37, 66, 89–90; in 1991–2004 phase, 26–27, 30; as hybrid weapon for Russia, 89–90, 125
"neighborhood policy" of Russia, 31
Neutralist Aid: during BiH war, 56–57, 68; *vs.* Interventionist Aid, 21, 67–69, 75–77
non-governmental aid, 17–18, 75; bilateral donor prominence over NGOs/international orgs and, 112–115; in Ukrainian War *vs.* Bosnian conflict, 65, 74–76. *See also* Neutralist Aid

oligarchy, Ukrainian, 30; anti-oligarch law, 41
Orange Revolution, 31, 38
Orić, Naser, 63

pacifist messages, 56
Pandemic Aid, 3–5, 85; political aspects of, 20; United Nations (UN) unpreparedness, 113–114; *Vaccine Diplomacy* and, 19–20, 73–74, 89; Western reactions to, 1–3. *See also* Interventionist Aid *vs.* Pandemic Aid
Partnership and Cooperation Agreement (PCA), EU and Ukraine and, 28–29, 32
peculiarities: in Aid to Ukraine (1991–2021), 5–8, 11–12, 21, 25, **71**; in Aid to Ukraine *vs.* BiH war, 21, 65–67; donor-recipient peculiarities, 65; eight peculiarities of Interventionist Aid, 21, 70–108, **71**, 92, 116, 121; EU and NATO and, 114; Interventionist Aid *vs.* Pandemic Aid and, 110, 114, 116, **118**, 129; of Russian aid (1991–2004 phase), 26–27, 30;

strategic approach peculiarities, 66–67; technical-political peculiarities of Ukrainian aid, 68, 96, 99, 121, 124
political obligation, donor-recipient, 4, 19
Poroshenko, Petro, 37
Post-democracy Aid: as potential future impact of Interventionist Aid, 10, 133–136
Powell, Colin, 33
Prighozin, Evgenij, 63
Prilić, Jadranko, 105
Pro-European Ambition Phase (2005–2010), 6, 25; Association Agreement (AA, EU-Ukraine) and, 32; EU interest in Ukrainian judiciary reform during, 33; EU-Ukrainian Action Plan of *European Neighborhood Policy* (ENP) and, 32; Orange Revolution and, 31; pro-Russian coinciding with pro-Western positions during, 34; TACIS program and, 33; Ukraine's joining of *Declaration of Aid Effectiveness* (2007), 34; US support of Yushchenko during, 33–34; USAID and Rule of Law strengthening during, 33
pro-Russian Kyiv governments, 5, 24–25; from 1991–2004, 31; coinciding with pro-Western positions in 2005–2010, 34; to eastern regions post-Crimea annexation, 44; Russia aid embracement in 2013, 37; withdrawal of post-Crimea annexation, 6, 38; Yanukovych dual-track policy and (2010–2014), 35, 37
pro-Russian regionalism in Eastern Ukraine, 31, 38
pro-Western Kyiv governments, 5, 24–25; from 2005–2010, 31–33; Association Agreement (AA, EU-Ukraine) and, 32, 38–39; coinciding with pro-Russian positions in 2005–2010, 34; EU/NATO membership and, 26, 42–44; military cooperation programs post-Crimea annexation and, 43–44; post-Maidan revolution, 37–38, 40; Tymosheko trial in 2012 and, 37
Putin, Vladimir, 88, 105

raw materials, 66, 89–90; as hybrid weapon for Russia, 89–90, 125; as Russian aid to Ukraine (1991–2004 phase), 26–27, 30; as Russian aid to Ukraine (2005–2010 phase), 34
Ražnatović, Željko ("Arkan"), 63
Reagan Administration, 54
realist theoretical approach in study of IAPPs, 8, 11–12, 19–22, **121**, 122, 124–128
Recipient-Driven Aid, **71**; *vs.* Donor-Recipient Partnership, **121**, 123–124; Interventionist Aid and, 8; media coverage and, 79–81; peculiarities of Kyiv's equal partnership in, 77–81; sanctions as, 67; shift from Donor-Driven to Recipient-Driven, 79–81
reconstruction of Ukraine post-conflict: donor competition over, 99–101; premature opening of, 96–99
"Re-framing Foreign Aid History and Politics," 4, 11
response speed of inter-state aid to Ukraine, 7, 65, 70–74, **71**, 116
Rule of Law: EU agenda of during 2014–2022, 38–39; U.S. agenda of during 2005–2010, 33–34; U.S. agenda of during 2010–2014, 36–37; Western principles of *vs.* tactical needs in sanctions, 106–108

Russia: "neighborhood policy" of, 31; citizens leaving to avoid military service, 108; Commonwealth of Independent States (CIS) Charter of, 31; divorce of multilateral cooperation by, 90–91; military aid to from China, India, Iran, 118; narrative of defense in decision to invade Ukraine by, 95; pro-Russian regionalism in Eastern Ukraine, 31, 38; Vaccine Diplomacy of, 2, 89, 115; Western bilateral aid/ donors primary objective of repelling, 7, 65, 67–68, 70–74, **71**, 116; Western/Ukrainian sanctions on, 104–107, 124, 132

Russian aid: in 1991–2004 phase, 6, 26–27, 30; during *Aid without Reforms Phase* (1991–2004), 26–27; divorce from multilateral cooperation of, 90–91; embracing of in 2013, 37; invasion of Ukraine as renunciation of Re-emerging Donor role, 12, 66, 88–91; post-Crimea (2014), 44; Russia aid embracement in 2013, 37, 89; unchallenged influence in coexistence phase (1994–2004), 6, 25–26; Vaccine Diplomacy of, 89. *See also* Russian *Weaponization of Aid*

Russian *Weaponization of Aid*, 125–126; classic aid goods as hybrid weapon, 7, 9, 66, 68, 125; as constituent element of Interventionist Aid, 12, 68–69, 117, 125; defined, 9, 68; food as a weapon in, 91–92; lack of shared agreement of new modalities, 117–118; lack of shared donor agreement on new modalities of action in, 117–118; as response to sanctions, 89; Russian divorce from multilateral cooperation and, 90–91; as war tactic, 90–91; Western criticism of, 117, 120, 127

sanctions, 118, **121**; on Bosnia, 105, 108; EU on Russia in 2014, 115; as recipient-driven, 106; recipient-driven sanctions, 106; Russian *Weaponization of Aid* in response to, 89; sanctions as aid, 7–8, 67, 103–108, 126; Western Rule of Law principles *vs.* tactical needs in, 106–108; Western/Ukrainian on Russia, 104–107, 124, 132

Saudi Arabian, new partnerships of, 112, 132
Scholz, Olaf, 79–80
solidarity for Ukraine, 96
Sputnik-V vaccine, 2, 89, 115; Western opposition to, 2
State Programme for Prevention and Combating Corruption, 36
Steinmeier, President (Germany), 80
Stoltenberg, Jens, 84, 113
Success-Oriented Aid, **121**, 122

TACIS program, 28–29, 33
Tito, Josip Broz, 50
Transition Aid: Interventionist Aid as overcoming historical, 9, 129–130, 132, 136
Tymosheko, Prime Minister Yulia, 37

Ukraine 2022 *vs.* Bosnia and Herzegovina 1992, 4–6; aid peculiarities in, 21, **49**, 65–66; civilian *vs.* military casualties, 64; classic military *vs.* ethnic-based paramilitary dynamics, 63–64; compared with Interventionist Aid *vs.* Pandemic Aid, 120; consolidated statehood/

diplomatic networks and, 62–63; Dayton Peace Accords and, 62, 99, 105; differential impact of on inter-state aid, 1–5; domestic/international context of BiH war and, 48, 50–55; donor-recipient peculiarities, 65; EU membership proposals and, 98–99; geo-political *vs.* humanitarian concerns and, 1–3, 67–69, 73–77, 85, 93–94; historical characteristics for comparison, 48, 50; international relevance/media exposure, 58–61, 70; military *vs.* humanitarian aid and, 93–94; Neutralist *vs.* Interventionist Aid, 67–69, 75–77; origins of conflict, 61, 72–73; political consequences of NGO/international aid during BiH war, 55–56, 75–76; sanctions and, 105, 108; strategic approach peculiarities, 66–67; systemic causes of difficulties in aid dispersion in BiH war, 56–57; travel difficulties by foreign leaders and, 79; Western bilateral donor response speed and commitment, 64–65, 70–74; Western presence/interest prior to conflict, 61–62, 71–72; Western reactions and, 1–3

Ukraine war (2022): historical-political relevance of, 4–5, 9–10, 111–112; impact on inter-state aid *vs.* Pandemic aid, 1–5; Interventionist Aid as effect of, 3–5, 12, 76, 86, 126; non-endorsement of by authors, 12–13; past aid to Ukraine as historical early symptom of, 5, 21; positive international visibility on, 80; as redefining international relations, 15, 112, 133; as turning point in inter-state aid, 1–3, 21, 92. *See also* Aid to Ukraine (1991–2021); Interventionist Aid; Ukraine 2022 vs. Bosnia and Herzegovina 1992; Western bilateral aid/donors in Ukraine 2022

Ukrainian government: autonomy of, 80–81; Crimea annexation as break point in pro-Western *vs.* pro-Russian alliances, 6, 38; as equal partner/sole recipient of Western bilateral aid, 7–8, 65, **71**, 72, 77–82, 105–106, 124; EU membership for Ukraine proposals, 26, 42–43, 66, 98–99, 101–103; post-conflict intervention discussions with, 96–97; pro-Russian regionalism in Eastern Ukraine, 31, 38; sanctions as aid and, 105–106; sanctions on Russia and, 104–107, 124, 132; Western Vaccine diplomacy and, 5. *See also* pro-Russian Kyiv governments; pro-Western Kyiv governments

United Nations (UN), 91; in BiH war, 53, 55, 76, 93, 105; failure of to mediate Ukraine War 2022, 75–76, 114–115; FAO, 91; overshadowing of by bilateral donors, 112–113; UNDP, 86; UNHCR, 55, 86; unpreparedness of for Covid-19 pandemic, 113–114; WHO, 1, 14, 113

United States: "preventive intervention" as dangerous concept, 95; geopolitical shifts and, 11, 137; military aid to Ukraine, 83–84; as second largest donor to Ukraine, 33; Ukraine integration into NATO and, 26; USAID and conditions of Rule of Law focus during 2010–2014, 36–37; USAID and Rule of Law focus during 2005–2010, 33–34; USAID during 1991–1995, 29; USAID during 2001–2004 and, 29–30; visits to Kyiv and BiH by leaders of, 79; Zelensky's visit to *vs.* Karzai's, 81–82. *See also* NATO; Western *Aidization of weapons*

Vaccine Diplomacy, 2, 19, 73–74; geo-political interests/ competition in, 117, 119–120; international relations and, 19–20; Interventionist Aid *vs.* Pandemic Aid and, 19–20, 73–74, 115, 117; in Italy, 2, 117; Russian, 2, 89, 115; of West *vs.* Russia, 1–3, 20; Western opposition to Sputnik-V vaccine, 2
Vatican, 82
Von Clausewitz, Carl, 126

Wagner Group, 63
War of Aid Phase (2010–2014), 6, 25; Association Agreement (AA, EU-Ukraine) suspension by Brussels, 37; Russia aid embracement in 2013, 37, 89; USAID and conditions of Rule of Law focus during 2010–2014, 36–37; Western anti-corruption and judiciary reform agenda during, 35–37; Yanukovych dual-track policy and, 35, 37
war, aid during, 85–88
war, author's rejection of, 12–13
Weaponization of Aid: defined, 9, 68. *See also* Russian *Weaponization of Aid*
Western aid: economic cooperation emphasis *vs.* liberal-democratic development, 6, 25–27, 30, 35–36
Western *Aidization of weapons*, 7, 66, 68, 92–96; as constituent element of Interventionist Aid, 12, 68–69, 117, 125; lack of shared donor agreement on new modalities of action in, 117–118; Russian criticism of, 117, 120, 127. *See also aidization of weapons*; military aid and training
Western bilateral aid/donors in Ukraine 2022: *vs.* in BiH war, 64–65; donor-recipient peculiarities in, 65; as containing Russian invasion, 83, 111, 119; geo-political *vs.* humanitarian concerns, 1–3, 7, 65–69, 73–77, 83, 85, 93–97; large quantity of diversified aid, 7, 66, 75, 82–88, 125; leading role and primacy of, 7, 65, 70–71, **71**, 74–77; leading role as defining primary objective of repelling Russia, 7, 65, 67–68, 70–74, **71**, 116; military aid and training, 83–87, 92–96; peculiarities of aid in, 6–8; premature discussion of Ukraine EU membership, 98–99; premature opening of post-war reconstruction, 7, 66, 96–98; relegation of humanitarian aid and, 7, 65–69, 73, 83, 85, 96–97; response speed of inter-state aid, 7, 64–65, 70–74, **71**, 116; sanctions as aid, 7–8, 67, 103–108; scale of vaccine diplomacy *vs.* aid at outbreak of war, 1–3; Ukrainian government as equal partner and sole recipient, 7–8, 65, **71**, 72, 77–82, 105–106, 123–124; *Vaccine Diplomacy* and, 19–20, 73–74; weapons as primary aid *(aidization of weapons)*, 7, 12, 66, 92–96. *See also* aid during wartime; military aid and training; Ukraine war (2022)
wheat, as hybrid weapon, 91, 117

World Disorder, 11, 15
World War Aid, as potential future impact of Interventionist Aid, 10–11, 136–138

Yanukovich, Viktor, 6, 24, 31; dual-track policy of (2010–2014), 35, 37; *Party of Regions of*, 34

Zelensky, President Volodymyr, 37, 40, 78, 81; European visit of, 81–82; political confidence of in visit to U.S. *vs.* Karzai's, 81–82

For Product Safety Concerns and Information please contact our EU
representative GPSR@taylorandfrancis.com
Taylor & Francis Verlag GmbH, Kaufingerstraße 24, 80331 München, Germany

www.ingramcontent.com/pod-product-compliance
Lightning Source LLC
Chambersburg PA
CBHW051747230426
43670CB00012B/2193